MW01194940

Management of New Product Launches and Other Marketing Projects

Michael W. Lodato Ph.D.

authorHOUSE®

AuthorHouse™
1663 Liberty Drive, Suite 200
Bloomington, IN 47403
www.authorhouse.com
Phone: 1-800-839-8640

© 2008 Michael W. Lodato Ph.D. All Rights Reserved.

No part of this book may be reproduced, stored in a retrieval system, or transmitted by any means without the written permission of the author.

First published by AuthorHouse September 19, 2008

ISBN: 978-1-4343-9084-4

Printed in the United States of America
Bloomington, Indiana

This book is printed on acid-free paper.

Management of New Product Launches and Other Marketing Projects

By

Michael W. Lodato Ph.D.

President
MWL & Company
32038 Watergate Court
Westlake Village, CA 91361 USA
(818) 889-7158
mwlodato@sbcglobal.net
www.marketingandsalesdoctor.com

Dedication

To Sylvia, my wife and best friend for 49 years.

To our four children, Laura, Jill, Kathryn and Mike, and

To our six grandchildren, Justin, Dale, Carly, Nick, Tim and Monica. I hope the dogs, chickens and other pets of these people aren't upset by not being mentioned.

I also dedicate this book to those many people with whom I have worked on projects during my career. In particular I am indebted to John Toellner, the creator of the Spectrum Project Management methodology. You will find many of his ideas in this book.

Glenn Craig was also one that worked with the Spectrum product. He brought to my knowledge the reality of what users really needed to manage projects better.

I also include Les Haentzschel in this dedication. Together we conducted twelve two-week long training programs for AT&T on *Management of Communication Systems Marketing Projects*. This was my realization that project management can be applied to marketing and sales.

Table of Contents

5. Project execution process

6. Controlling the project

7. Product Launch Management

About the Author
Michael W. Lodato, Ph.D.

Michael W. Lodato Ph.D. is an accomplished expert in virtually every facet of marketing and sales, with over 40 years experience as a company president, senior executive, Associate Professor at California Lutheran University, and as a consultant to dozens of companies in the U.S. and Europe.

His focus is to regard marketing and sales as a set of processes to be integrated, managed and improved over time. It is from this vantage point that Dr Lodato has become a prolific author of books, booklets and other educational materials. He is the developer of

- *Integrated Sales Process Management,*
- *Integrated Territory Management,*
- *Integrated Channel Management,* and
- *The MASTER Method of Selling.*

Dr. Lodato worked with clients in developing and implementing structured processes for sales management, strategic management, and product marketing management. His uniquely effective processes have been implemented at companies in the US and Europe and are now available in publications to those desiring to improve the performance of their marketing and sales teams.

Dr. Lodato's books, booklets, white papers and articles provide in-depth insight and detailed understanding into how to construct, improve and manage all aspects of marketing and sales activity. His full length books:

- *Integrated Sales Process Management: a methodology for improving sales effectiveness in the 21st Century*
- *Selling Computers and Software: the MASTER Method*
- *Management of New Product Launches and Other Marketing Projects*

are available from the publisher site and other sources including amazon.com, Barnes & Nobel, Borders and local book stores.

Descriptions of shorter-length publications can be found on his website www.marketingandsalesdoctor.com.

Michael's success with clients has made a case for a business process orientation to how a company's marketing and sales activities are managed - so that their performance can be consistently and repeatedly improved over time.   With his insightful, effective methods to this challenging area, a company has a very good shot at achieving true best practice level of performance in this vital area.

Michael is an avid golfer and has degrees from Colgate University (B.A.), the University of Rochester (M.S.), and Rutgers (Ph.D.).

1. Sales and marketing projects

The jobs of sales and marketing are both routine and project type. There is enough important sales and marketing work that is time *specific* and produces *specific* products, systems or other deliverables, that it should be managed as a project. Examples are

- New product launches, (covered in Chapter 7), where a lot of *specific* things – including the product, the support program, and promotion - have to be completed by a *specific* date – the launch target date
- promotion campaigns, where *specific* ads, brochures, TV spots, etc. have to be placed by *specific* dates
- recruiting of channel partners, where *specific* agreements need to be signed with *specific* companies to be business partners within a *specific* time frame
- the sale of a *specific* offering to a *specific* prospect or customer

On-going or routine activity, such as customer support, weekly status reporting and analysis of the competition, does not require management as projects. It is our conviction that success in performing sales and marketing work is enhanced when formal project management methodology is consistently applied.

Yet not many sales and marketing personnel get exposed to training or guidance in project management and so are ill equipped to perform well on these important tasks. This book has been written to help marketing and sales people develop strong project management capabilities. This is what the reader will find in the rest of this book:

Chapter 2, *Management and Management Processes*, sets a proper context for performing project management work.

Chapter 3, *Project Management,* discusses management of projects that are encountered in sales and marketing.

Chapter 4, *The Project Planning Process,* provides detailed guidance in the planning of marketing and sales projects. It shows how to define the tasks needed to be done, how to put them in the proper sequence and how long each task should take.

Chapter 5, *The Project Execution Process,* leads the reader in deciding on the proper organization and relationship of resources and processes to

1

achieve the plan objectives, locating and getting all resources and processes needed to achieve the goals, and directing, coordinating, synchronizing, and symphonizing resources in changing and dynamic environments.

Chapter 6, *Controlling the Project,* discusses measuring and monitoring actual performance and providing direction when expectations are not being met. The discussion covers the concept of control, outlines quality reviews, distinguishes between calendar-driven and event-driven control, and describes time and progress reporting.

Chapter 7, *Product Launch Management,* details how to apply the previous six chapters to managing new product launches. Readers will get an appreciation of the magnitude of the product launch challenge and will develop a confidence that, with the tools provided, they can overcome these challenges.

You will find a very ample list of launch program tasks and see how they are related in work breakdown structures. Further, there is a set of *Launch Readiness Checklists* and instructions for how to use them to control product launch projects.

At the end of Chapter 7 are guidelines for using the *Launch Readiness Checklists* methodology as a product launch audit tool.

The book contains all the elements needed to plan, execute and control sales and marketing projects.

2. Management and Management Processes

Introduction

In recent years a lot of attention has been given to business process management (BPM). I've been toiling in the area for over three decades and I've written over 1000 pages on the subject. The core process of BPM is *management*, which is discussed in detail in this chapter. Hopefully the precision in definitions and illustrations contained herein will help bring more understanding of management and its place in the study and application of BPM.

A goal of management is to provide desired results effectively and efficiently. This is done through the use of *resources* in specific *applications* or *contexts*. In each situation, there are five management activities in play:

- *Planning* – identifying and deciding what to do and how to do it. Planning activities provide goals and expectations.
- *Implementing* – consisting of the following three sub-activities:
  - o *Arranging* – deciding on the proper organization and relationship of resources and processes to most efficiently and effectively achieve the desired results or outcomes, i.e. the plan objectives
  - o *Sourcing* – locating and getting all resources and processes needed to achieve the goals.
  - o *Orchestrating* – directing, coordinating, synchronizing, and symphonizing resources in changing and dynamic environments.
- *Control* – measuring and monitoring actual performance, comparing it to expectations, evaluating differences and providing direction for adjusting arranging, sourcing and orchestrating activities or changes to the plan.

In every case the five primary management activities are applied to *resources* in an *application* or *context*.

3

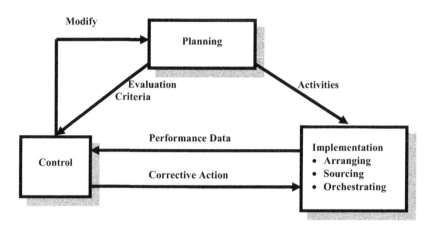

The 5 Primary Management Activities and Their Relationships

My understanding of management was significantly advanced by reading a paper I stumbled upon while attending a business conference in Athens in 2003. The paper, *Management and Leadership for 21st Century Leaders,* is by Michael Klimesh. What you find in this paper is an articulation of what management is that is strongly influenced by Klimesh.

The differences in the sets of *resources* applied and the *applications* or *contexts* in which they are applied make kinds or forms of management different from one another. And so, marketing management is different from production management because it uses a different set of resources than production management and applies them in a different context. There are many different kinds of management, including people management, time management, financial management, information management, asset management, sales management, outsourcing management, energy management, leisure management, risk management, administrative management, systems management and more

Having a plan is crucial to management. The other four activities are not possible without a plan. Referring to the *control* activity, Klimesh says, "Having a plan says there are expectations, targets, standards, or desires. Monitoring and measuring performance yields information about what is actually happening." It tells us the degree to which expectations, targets, standards or desires are being met or unmet. This is the basis for the *control* activity. Differences are analyzed and evaluated to determine the root causes of unmet expectations and decisions are made about what to do about the situation.

As indicated by the graphic above, there are two potential courses of action:

1. Make changes to the
    *   *Arranging,*
    *   *Sourcing,* and/or
    *   *Orchestrating* and/or
2. Modify the *plan.*

Changes to the arranging might involve making changes to processes, which may not be as appropriate as thought earlier. In other words, the processes as well as the activities need to be managed.

A 3-dimensional view of management

The 3-dimensional graphic (from the Klimesh paper), shown below, illustrates that management *activities* are applied to *resources* in a *context.* The small cube below represents one of the cubes that could be in the interior of the graphic – *arranging facilities* for a new *distribution* center.

Resources

The answer to the question "What is managed?" is 'resources are managed'. Resources have qualitative and quantitative values. Resources include people, money or capital, machines, facilities, materials, energy, information, time, proximity, intellectual property, technology, and a whole lot more.

Applications or Contexts

The number of application contexts is almost limitless. Here are a few: business, personal, domestic, civic, leisure, technical, manufacturing, marketing, sales, distribution, medical and promotion. You can get very specific about the contexts, for example, *Michael's restaurant,* instead of business or the *New York Police Department*, instead of civic.

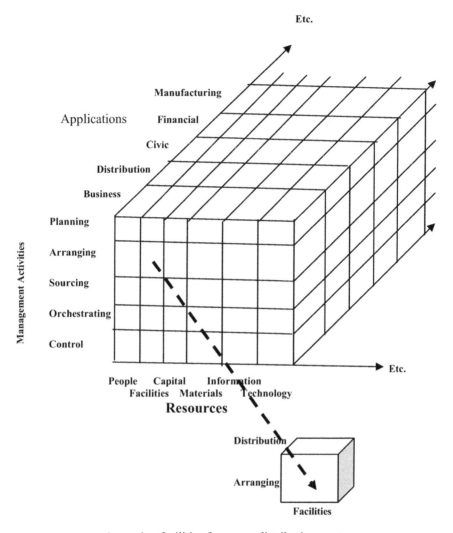

Arranging facilities for a new distribution center

The use of etc. suggests that the lists of applications and resources can be expanded as appropriate to each situation. The number of applications/contexts and resources are limited only by the circumstances and the needs of the situation.

Management is exercised in a context

Here are some dimensions of the context in which management is exercised
- Situational
- Commitment

- Communication
- Teamwork
- Responsibility/accountability
- Authority

Situational has to do with circumstances of time, place, culture, (beliefs, ethics, practices, traditions), politics, society, and economics.

What is the situational and circumstantial context in which a campus restaurant is managed? Included in the answer are its location, hours of operation that depend on when students are on campus, a tie-in with the cafeteria program, whether or not alcohol is allowed, faculty discounts, the department that has responsibility for the restaurant, how it relates to other departments and much more.

Management is exercised at many levels. A department is managed within a division and the division becomes part of the context of the department's management. Departments interact with other departments at the same level and those other departments become part of the context.

Commitment is the personal motivation and attitude of devotion to the needs and goals to be achieved. It is fostered and nurtured by the environment. Commitment has personal, organizational and environmental dimensions:

- Compensation and other rewards are essential to motivation
- A positive environment contributes to motivation
- Motivated people contribute to a positive motivational environment
- Committed people are proud of what they are and what they do.

We can all give examples of people with commitment – Mother Theresa, a US Marine, most top athletes who must be committed to fitness, practice, strategy, and concentration, etc

Commitment is much more than involvement, as illustrated by the typical American breakfast.

The chicken was involved, the pig was <u>committed</u>

<u>Communication</u> is the process of conveying and making meaning understood through information, instructions, illustrations, body language, and so on. It is a two-way street. Listening, receiving and understanding the meaning are crucial. Communication is also multi-directional – going up and down and sideways. One-way, unilateral communication is not a part of effective management. The goal to is get the right information and understanding to the right people by the most appropriate channels at the right time, and in the right formats. Without such communication much time is wasted and productivity damaged when people don't know what they can expect, when they can expect it, and from whom they should expect it. Communication cannot be effective without trust.

Sales management effectiveness is dependent upon communication between salespeople and their managers and among members of a sales team. Coaching is a form of communication found in better sales organizations.

<u>Teamwork</u> is co-operation among members of a group. A group is not a team; it is an assembly of people that come together. We are all aware of the importance of teamwork in sports and the consequences of ineffective teamwork. If we think about it we can also easily be convinced of the importance of teamwork in a management situation. Team members cannot work together without communication. Communication is through instruction and responses. Teamwork is the action. Without good communication teamwork fails.

<u>Responsibility</u> is being accountable, trustworthy and rational. People are vested with responsibility. Without people accepting responsibility at all levels, the management effort lacks direction and there is no court of last resort. Responsibility means being accountable and answerable for an outcome. It is assumed or assigned in organizations and can exist by virtue of position (Joe is responsibly for editing). Unless the person is given the

authority to exercise decision-making, the notion of responsibility is meaningless.

Authority is the right and/or obligation to determine, direct, judge, decide, and/or enforce. Authority must be granted and exercised for responsibilities to be performed. Responsibility belongs to the person to whom it is vested. Authority, the power to act, can be delegated or passed to another, but responsibility/accountability cannot.

A definition of management

The foregoing is a buildup to the following definition of management presented by Klimesh.

Management is
- *A situational system and processes*
- *Relying on and fostering commitment*
- *With sound communication and teamwork*
- *Based on assigned and accepted responsibility and exercised authority*
- *To achieve goals*
- *Using resources effectively and efficiently*
- *Through planning, arranging, sourcing, orchestrating and control*
- *To achieve results*
- *Through proper decision-making*

[Klimesh states that if at least these 19 underlined elements are not present in significant and deliberate measure whatever is happening is not management.]

If strategic leadership is developing the over-all big picture and direction, management is implementing and maintaining the strategic direction.

Definitions of some of the terms used above are
- *System = interconnection of elements and processes forming a complex whole*
- *Goals = the end results and expectations that are desired*
- *Effectiveness = did the actual performance satisfy objectives of expending resources?*
- *Efficient(ly) = with the best practical relationship of inputs to outputs*
- *Results = those outcomes that are achieved*
- *Decision making = the process of selecting from alternatives*

9

The point is that management is a system and processes working in an environment.

Decision making

Management is a decision-making activity.   Here is a process model for making decisions that I have used in my classes for years.

D1 → **D2** → **D3** → **D4** → **D5** → **D6** → **D7**

Situation	Problem or Opportunity	Develop Alternatives	Analyze Alternatives	Select Solution(s)	Implement & Modify	Control

These are steps to making **non-routine** decisions, where a more formal approach is appropriate. Routine decisions are usually made based on experience and judgment.

This type of *decision-making* is simply defined as *the process* of selecting from alternatives.   It exists whenever
- management is confronted with two or more courses of action to reach an objective, and
- uncertainty exists regarding the best course of action

Step **D1** - *Recognize a decision situation* - is almost self-explanatory. You recognize that you are confronted with a decision that will require some analysis and evaluation of alternatives.

For example, suppose your performance measures reveal that you have a product that isn't "cutting the mustard" – i.e., it is not meeting its revenue or profit goals.

Or you might have to decide whether or not to buy a time-share, or you may want to decide whether or not to go to graduate school.

In **D2** - D*efining the decision problem or opportunity* - there are two components
1. Understanding the objectives surrounding the decision situation
2. Statement of problems or opportunities present.

E.g., in the product not meeting expectations case, objectives might be
- To minimize losses
- Maintain customer satisfaction
- Protect the firm's reputation in the industry.

Decision makers are responsible for ensuring that the *decision* objectives are specified and problems and opportunities are clearly identified.

Problems could be from
- performance falling "out of tolerance"
- ineffective marketing program
- changes in situational factors (assumptions not being met)

Once a problem or opportunity is recognized, the main issues and causal factors need to be identified.

There are two components to defining the decision problems or opportunities
1. Analysis of existing information, such as
   - win/loss reports
   - analysis of potential causes of the problem:
     - ➤ being sold into the wrong markets
     - ➤ wrong features vs. the competition
     - ➤ poor positioning.

   A problem might be that market share is being lost, or there could be an opportunity to retain maintenance revenue
2. Employ *exploratory research* to help search for the causes of problems.

Exploratory research is the process of discussing a business problem with informed sources such as industry analysts, consultants, customers and channel partners and examining secondary sources of data.

This could involve purchase of buyer intention data from a research company. It could also involve conducting focus groups.

The decision can be no better than the best alternative under consideration. So in **D3** we identify alternative courses of action.

Some alternatives for the problem of a product not meeting expectations are
- Keep the product and
  - ➤ add or change features
  - ➤ change the target market
  - ➤ change positioning
  - ➤ etc.

- Drop the product by
  - ➤ selling it to another company
  - ➤ dropping it "cold turkey"
  - ➤ phasing it out over time

Michael W. Lodato Ph. D.

Exploratory research may help to identify innovative courses of action

D4 - *Analyze Alternatives* - is the point in the decision-making process where conclusive research is often employed to reduce uncertainty.

Conclusive research includes surveys, focus groups, observations, etc.

Here is a list of the steps in the conclusive research process that I have found very useful over the years

      R1. Establish need for information
      R2. Specify research objectives & information needs
      R3. Specify the research design & sources of data
      R4. Develop data collection procedures
      R5. Design the sample
      R6. Collect the data
      R7. Process the data
      R8. Analyze the data.
      R9. Present research results

I recommend this over the process presented in many textbooks. It is more intuitive and contains more steps.

We won't go through the steps here, in order to keep focus on management as a process. The effectiveness of the conclusive research process depends upon
- anticipation of all of the steps and
- recognition of their interdependencies

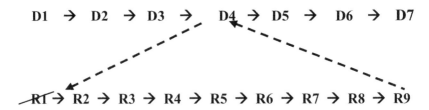

This graphic shows how the conclusive research process is the vehicle for evaluating alternative courses of action.

R1 is crossed out because the first three steps in the decision-making process will have established the need for the information.

Once the research results are submitted to the decision makers, a course of action is selected. This is done in step **D5.**

D6 - *Implement Solution* - is where the solution is activated, acceptance is gained and identification of what could go wrong is identified.

D7 – *Control* - is where managers stay in touch with the implementation and adjust performance or expectations as necessary. Often *performance monitoring research* is used to monitor the effectiveness of the course of action. It is a useful element to control implementation in accordance with plans

Processes

A *process* is a series of actions, changes, or functions bringing about a result. It consists of the steps between inputs and outputs. Processes require systemization. The elements of processes and systems are measurable and therefore controllable and changeable and improvable. This is an important point about processes.

A process consists of logically related activities or tasks and is aimed to achieve a certain result. If processes were not in evidence people would not be able to achieve desired results consistently.

Processes and systems are essential to the definition of management. Following processes is part of what management is all about. Without processes, management activities would be random and would not work together as a whole. But for true effectiveness, management processes must themselves be managed. Hence, we have the term process management. Processes need constant tweaking. One of the benefits of having a documented, structured process is that it makes it easier to improve them and to tailor them to different situations.

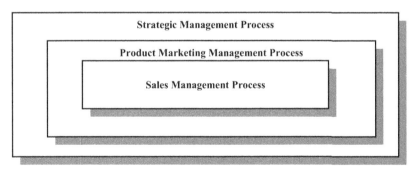

Strategic Management Process

Product Marketing Management Process

Sales Management Process

Management processes are nested

The figure above shows three business management processes. Notice the *nesting* of management processes, i.e., the sales management process is part of the (larger) product marketing management process, which in turn is a part of the (larger) strategic management processes. The figure could go on to deeper levels. For example, processes within the sales management process include the lead management process, opportunity management process, territory management process, account management process, and others, as illustrated in *Figure A* below.

The ***nesting*** shown in the above figure implies a strong integration among strategic, marketing and sales management processes. It is important that the integration among strategic, marketing and sales processes be seamless.

What is clear to me is that all management processes within a company are interrelated and inseparable. They all affect one another and function like a wheel. Assuming that the wheel is traveling in the right direction (strategy), if one discipline in the company is stronger or weaker than the others there is an imbalance in the execution of strategy (tactics) and the company never achieves its full potential.

For example, if marketing has correctly defined the market and the products, but sales fails to execute, engineering fails to design the products on time and within budget, or manufacturing fails to deliver a quality product at reasonable costs, then the company cannot succeed.

Sales and Marketing Plan

Sales Management Processes
Figure A

14

Figure A shows the set of sales management processes that are the components of an overall integrated sales management process. The arrows give an indication of how the processes are related and how information flows among them. For the overall integrated sales management process to be successful each of the components must be managed with a high degree of precision.

The connected set of sales management processes is the mechanism by which the sales and marketing plan is implemented.

Defining management processes

What we try to do in defining management processes is to identify and relate major activities or bits of effort and then break them down, level-by-level, until you arrive at activities or work elements that are *bite-sized*, that is, large enough to *chew on* (meaningful and assignable) yet small enough so that one does not *choke* on them. When such a work breakdown structure is done correctly, the work elements at each level are related to one another and to the work elements at higher and lower levels – just what you want for business process management.

The U.S. Armed Forces and NASA have used work breakdown structures successfully for decades in the development of very large weapon systems and space programs. There is a US Air Force Systems Command manual, AFSCM375-5 that the author used to define and relate project work elements in the 1960s when working on such large projects. One of the techniques, *functional flow block diagramming* (FFBD), is summarized below. An often used similar technique is the *Work Breakdown Structure (WBS)*.

Functional flow analysis technique for defining project work elements

During my career, I have been successful in determining the elements of work that make up a project and in structuring functional relationships among project parts through the use of *Functional Flow Block Diagramming*. I have applied FFBD when developing management processes and articulating process management – particularly related to marketing and sales.

Certain format rules and symbols have been developed but the main emphasis is on accuracy and completeness rather than format. We will use the term "function" throughout instead of "work element" or activity.

Michael W. Lodato Ph. D.

Function Numbering

- Functions are numbered for ease of reference and to show indentured relationships.
- Top-level functions are numbered 1.0, 2.0, etc
- Functions numbers are sequentially assigned for all levels below the top level to preserve functional continuity.
- Functions at lower levels contain the same parent identifier and are coded at the next decimal level for each indenture.
- All flows below the top level are indicated by a decimal extension – a further expansion of function 2.0 might result as follows:

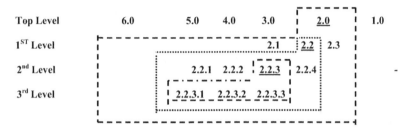

Function Block

- Each separate function is presented in a single box enclosed by a solid line.

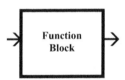

Function Reference

- Each functional diagram contains reference to its next higher functional diagram through the use of a reference block, which is a single box enclosed by dashed lines.

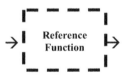

A reference function is part of another flow.

Flow Connection

- Lines connecting functions indicate only the functional flow.

- Vertical and horizontal lines between blocks indicate that all functions so interrelated are in either a parallel or series sequence as indicated.
- Diagonal lines are used to indicate alternative sequences (cases where alternative paths lead to the next function in the sequence.)

Flow Direction

- Functional diagrams are laid out so that functional flow is from left to right, and the reverse flow, in case of a functional loop, from right to left.

- Flow is shown from left to right and top to bottom unless a *feedback loop* is intended

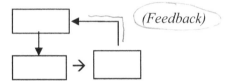

- Primary input lines enter the function block from the left side.
- Primary output or "GO" lines exit are from the right.
- "NO GO" lines exit from the bottom of the box.

GO-NO GO Paths

- The symbols **G** and **−G** are used to indicate GO or NO GO paths
- The symbols indicate alternative paths based on the success or failure of the function.
- GO flow indicates direction of flow if positive action is taken as a result of a functional decision or if the function is accomplished within system tolerances.

- NO GO flow indicates direction of flow if negative action is taken as a result of a functional decision or if the function is outside system tolerances.

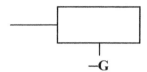

–G

- Whenever a GO flow notation is used, it implies a NO GO condition is possible or visa-versa. There must always be a set of **G** and **–G** flows

Summing Gates

- *A circle* **O** *is used to depict a summing gate.*
- A summing gate indicates the convergence or divergence of parallel or alternative functional paths and is annotated with the terms AND or OR

- **AND** indicates that parallel functions leading into the gate must be accomplished before proceeding to the next function

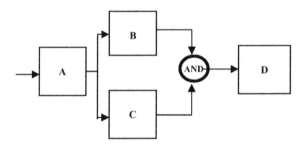

Parallel functions **B** and **C** are performed after the completion of function **A**. Function **D** cannot be performed until both functions **B** and **C** have been completed.

- **OR** indicates that any one of several alternative paths converge to the OR gate.

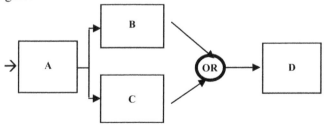

Two alternative functions **B** and **C** are shown. Function **D** may be performed if either **B** or **C** has been completed.

Advantages of the FFBD Approach

- It encourages and facilitates communication among operational managers, project managers, project workers, and users. It is easier to structure dialog and keep it from straying off course when you relate the discussions to a graphic of this type.
- Users appreciate the systemization of their functions and are encouraged that they can increase the analysts' or project workers' understanding so easily.
- It adds to the comprehensiveness of the analysis. Once functions are related, as indicated, at each level, the analyst or project worker and users can examine the diagram and usually identify functions that should be there because of the relationships that should exist.
- Functional analysis of any function or functional level is facilitated because they can be related in a larger context.
- Functions are easily related to goals.
- Alternative methods of performing a function or task at any level are easily identified.
- A functional flow block diagram acts as a common denominator for comparison with existing (or other) systems.

Creating functional flow block diagrams

A functional analysis utilizing the functional flow block diagramming technique usually proceeds as in the following paragraphs.

Here is an actual example that shows my application of the technique to a project of developing and conducting a course in Marketing Management. I was invited to conduct such a course at a university in Germany in the summer of 2003.

Top-level functions were identified and related. These identities and relationships are represented by a top-level functional flow (See below). A good practice when drawing functional flows is to define functions from the end (right) and back toward the reference box (left). Assign the box numbers after you have drawn and placed the boxes.

Example: Development and Delivery of a Marketing Management Course

Michael W. Lodato Ph. D.

TOP LEVEL

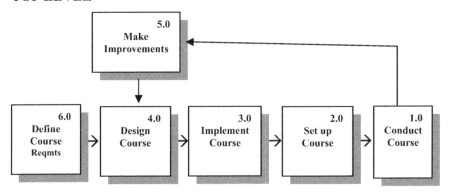

Example of Top Level Functional Flow Diagram

FIRST LEVEL

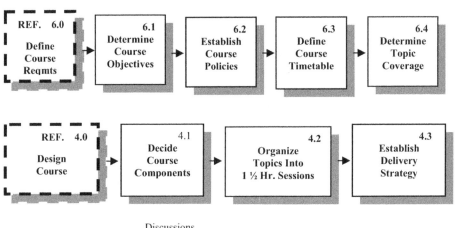

Discussions
Tests
Projects

FIRST LEVEL (Continued)

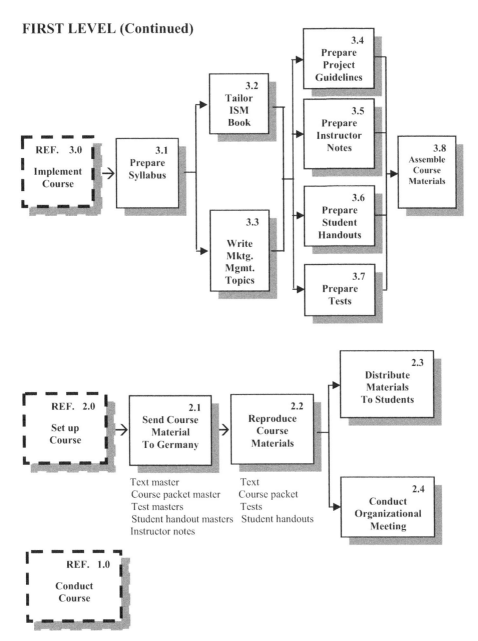

The functions at the first level seem to be *chewable bites* of work (as defined later) and so no second level breakdowns were prepared. I have made some notes under three of the boxes to explain them further.

As a summary, here is a procedure for using Functional Flow Block Diagramming for defining management processes.

1. Divide the overall management process into phases or stages as I have done in the above example. The top level of an FFBD should fulfill this step.
2. Create first level flows.
3. If necessary, create lower level flows for each block in the first level flow. Define "products" or "deliverables" from each lower level block.
4. Identify specific work steps to create the deliverables. Reiterate.
5. Group work steps into tasks, if they already aren't at a task level.
6. Define logical relationships among deliverables and tasks. That is, indicate which steps have to be done in a given sequence and which tasks can be done in parallel. Reiterate

The creation of lower level flows gives evidence of the "nesting" of business management processes and helps to recognize the vertical relationships among the processes. We must also seek to identify and describe horizontal relationships with other processes at the same level.

Finally, recognize that management processes must themselves be managed and changed or updated when necessary. **You should not let your organization be a fixed system of rules and processes based on what worked in the past.**

3. Project Management

Introduction

$\mathbf{A}$ project is different than routine work. Projects produce *specific* products, systems or other results by a *specific* target date – usually within a *specific* budget. Routine work is on going. Maintaining the garden is routine; the creation of the garden is often called a landscaping project.

> *There is nothing more difficult to plan, more doubtful of success, nor more dangerous to manage than the creation of a new system. For the initiator has the enmity of all who would profit by the preservation of the old system and merely lukewarm defenders in those who would gain by the new one*
> **Machiavelli, 1513**

The challenges of successfully completing a project have been apparent for centuries as implied by the accompanying box.

This chapter discusses management of projects that are encountered in sales and marketing.

Projects	Routine Work
Definite beginning and end	No beginning and end
Temporary in nature	On-going
Unique product or service	Products the same over and over
Dedicated resources to the project	Resources dedicated to on-going operations
Ending determined by specific criteria	Processes are not completed

Problems of Project Management and Their Causes

$\mathbf{H}$ere is a list of common problems of project management with their associated causes

Problem: Cost overruns
Causes:

- Work breakdown is too gross
- *Fudge factors* being used instead of explicit environmental factors
- Management won't *buy* realistic estimates
- Only one estimate is made
- *Ballooning* scope
- Poor visibility on status
- Low productivity of the project team, (although this is rare)

Problem: Schedule slippages
Causes

- Poor estimating
- Imposed deadlines
- *Packing* the schedule
- Interdependencies among tasks
- Lack of clear task guidance
- *Borrowing* resources from the project team
- Project team turnover.

> **The project completion date is not an input**

[**A Note about Imposed Schedules and Schedule Slippages.** One of the project management rules I've always followed is *The project completion date is not an input*. The completion date must be determined with full recognition of the scope of the resulting product or system, the resources that will be committed to the project and the quality standards that will be followed. Let us suppose that a project plan is developed that takes into account each of these issues and has come up with a *Planned Completion Date*.

Now, let us suppose that management finds fault with the *Planned Completion Date* and imposes a completion date that is 3 months earlier than the *Planned Completion Date*. If the plan was done with integrity, the *Imposed Completion Date* can only be met if the scope is reduced, additional resources are added, or quality standards are compromised. Usually, management or the customer doesn't want to reduce the scope and no one is in favor of reducing quality standards. That leaves the addition of resources as the only alternative.

But adding people doesn't always help. Two people on a task designed for one person doesn't cut the task duration in half especially if the additional person isn't as skilled or knowledgeable as the first. Even if the new person is of equal talent the communications overhead comes into play and the task can actually take as long, or longer, than when done as planned. Finally, some things just can't be hurried. Also, we have to contend with the false assumption that everything will go well.]

Problem: User dissatisfaction
Causes:

- Management not holding users accountable for success
- Lack of an effective project organization.
- Users role not explicit – especially relative to quality reviews
- Ineffective capturing of user requirements
- Lack of strong user commitment

Problem: Poor documentation
Causes:
- Incomplete documentation standards
- Postponement of documentation
- Lack of enforcement of standards
- Indecision on when and how to review document quality

Problem: Excessive rework
Causes
- No restrictions on jumping ahead
- Lack of clear guidance
- Project plan and development philosophy unclear
- Shallow, report-oriented user requirements definition

Problem: Over-reliance on senior people
Causes:
- No written guidelines
- Time needed for training
- Lack of task structure and checklists
- Inadequate standards
- *Spotty* documentation

For projects to produce software systems, we add

Problem: Poor software quality
Causes:
- Incomplete standards
- Poorly done quality reviews
- Poor test planning
- Inadequate test data
- Incomplete systems testing
- Lack of effective policies

We can avoid these problems if we:
- Define the work explicitly
- Make responsibilities clear
- Provide all needed inputs
- Estimate realistically and make schedules feasible
- Re-estimate and re-schedule regularly
- Have reviews at key milestones
- Insist on regular status reports
- Control changes
- Have a clean turnover (conclusion)

Overview of Project Management

Project management *is the set of policies, procedures, guidelines, forms, check lists, etc. used to achieve <u>goals</u>, related to a specific problem or opportunity, using <u>resources</u> <u>effectively</u> and <u>efficiently</u>, through <u>planning</u>, <u>arranging</u>, <u>sourcing</u>, <u>orchestrating</u> and <u>controlling</u>*

The objectives of project management are to do this on time, within budget and with high quality. The saying is, "Do it right the first time".

The following figure shows the five major activities of project management and how they are related.

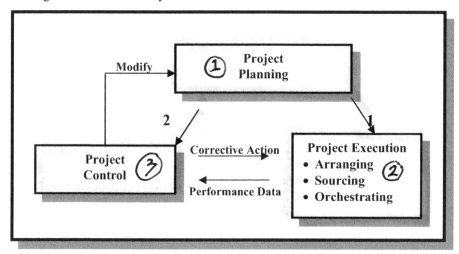

<u>Project planning</u> deals with identifying and deciding what should be done and how it should be done. In the above illustration, **1** indicates that project planning specifies the project activities and **2** indicates that project planning specifies the control activities and the control criteria.

<u>Project execution</u> consists of 3 activities:
- <u>Arranging</u> – Deciding on the proper organization and relationships of resources and processes to most effectively and efficiently achieve the desired results or outcomes - the project objectives
- <u>Sourcing</u> – Locating and obtaining all resources needed
- <u>Orchestrating</u> – Directing, coordinating, synchronizing, and symphonizing resources in changing and dynamic environments that are often experienced in projects

<u>Project controlling</u> – consists of measuring and monitoring actual performance, comparing it to expectations, evaluating differences and providing direction for adjusting implementation activities or changes to the plan.

The project control element receives performance data from the project execution element. If something is amiss and control determines that it is the result of an execution problem, corrective action is specified to the project execution element.

If project control determines that it is the result of an imperfect plan, directives to modify the plan are sent to the project planning activity.

Planning is crucial to management. The other 4 activities are not possible without a plan

Comparing actual performance to the plan will produce a difference or variance. Differences can be positive or negative, big or small.

Differences that are "out of tolerance" demand analysis and evaluation as to root causes. Then decisions are made about what to do

There are 2 possible courses of action:
1. Adjust the plan/expectations and/or
2. Take actions to change actual performance

The general sequence is important
1. Planning is undertaken
2. Project execution proceeds through
    - Arranging
    - Sourcing
    - Orchestrating
3. Controlling is applied

Elements of a Project Management Process

A project management process consists of five elements:

1. The *work breakdown* element, which specifies:
    - the products that are to be produced,
    - the tasks to be undertaken to produce those products and
    - the relationships among the products and tasks.

2. The *documentation* element, which provides the standards, forms, checklists and guidance for creating and maintaining project files.

3. The *phase management* element, which provides the processes for:
   - Planning the project, (including estimating and scheduling)
   - Arranging, sourcing and orchestrating the project execution and
   - Controlling the project.

4. The *change management* element, which provides the processes and techniques for handling:
   - Changes during the project and
   - Changes to existing systems

5. The *management control* element, which provides processes for measuring performance against expectations and either adjusting the plan or changing the arranging, sourcing or orchestrating.

Ingredients of a Successful Project

We can't always have a perfect situation when we conduct projects, but experience shows that projects tend to be successful when:

- A complete task structure exists and we know all the work that needs to be done.
- There is detailed task guidance
- There are standards for documentation and other project activity performance.
- There is strong commitment from management and the users of the project results.
- Good estimating tools are available and used.
- Quality and funding reviews are held throughout the project.
- Phased task releases are employed

> **Project management goal:**
> *Do it right the first time*

What a good project management methodology accomplishes

- Sales and marketing projects are completed on schedule and within their budgets
- Users will be deeply involved in the design and implementation of programs that impact their operations and pleased with the results.

- Visibility on where projects stand will be clear and up-to-date.
- Employee morale will rise.

Benefits to project workers of good project management

For project team members
- There is higher job satisfaction because the assignments are clear, the due dates are realistic and they get higher recognition for what they do.
- Career growth is enhanced because they experience and see the benefit of good planning and management.
- There are opportunities to utilize their creativity.
- Documentation is not as much of a chore because it is the natural by-product of tasks.
- The system that results is easier to maintain.

Benefits to the project manager include:
- Working against plans that are supportable and attainable.
- The amount of management time is reduced.
- Problems are anticipated before they are experienced.
- Change is easier to manage.
- In short, they build a high quality system on time and within budget **the first time.**

John Newbern's Law

People can be divided into three groups:
1. *Those who make things happen*
2. *Those who watch things happen,*
3. *Those who wonder what happened*

---

4. The Project Planning Process

*F*igure *1-A* shows the steps in the project planning process.

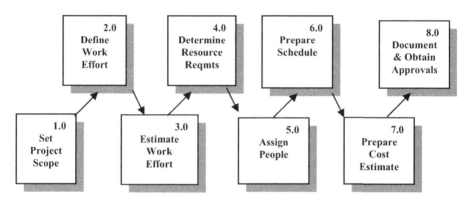

Figure 1-A: The Project Planning Process

Planning Step 1.0: Setting the project scope

The project scope gives the objectives, including the desired project outcomes, and constraints to be considered. It could include quality standards and customer expectations

This step also addresses the scope of the major output or product from the project. If the project is to produce a computer software system, the scope would describe how it would work, the features and functions, storage capacity, speed, maintainability, ease of use and other capabilities.

The scope of a new product launch project, discussed in Chapter 7, would describe the attributes of the product being launched; the amount of promotion that would be done, the people needs, and so forth.

Clarity is provided when statements about what will **not** be included are provided – for example, what the system will not accomplish.   Potential problems during development and operation might be mentioned as part of the scope.

It is important to document the project scope because, if the project should be running late, one of the remedies is a reduction to the scope of the project.

Planning Step 2.0: Defining the Project Work Effort

What we try to do in defining the project work effort is to identify and relate major bits of effort and then break them down, level-by-level, until we arrive at work elements that are *bite-sized*, that is, large enough to *chew on* (meaningful and assignable) yet small enough so one does not *choke* on them. When such a work breakdown structure is done correctly, the work elements at each level are related to one another and to the work elements at higher and lower levels.

In Chapter 2, the reader was introduced to one of the techniques for doing this: *functional flow block diagramming (FFBD)*. There you will find certain rules and symbols that have been developed for the technique. In my career I have used FFBD to determine elements of work that make up a project and in structuring functional relationships among project parts.

Chapter 2 also listed the advantages of using the FFBD approach and provided an example of applying it to the selling of a complex product.

In hopes that the material will be more understandable to the reader, I am relating application of the technique to the development of a sales cycle management process for sales of a complex product.

The process for selling a complex product - one where a solution is involved - often proceeds through 4 *stages*. The identities and relationships among the stages are represented by a top-level functional flow.

TOP LEVEL

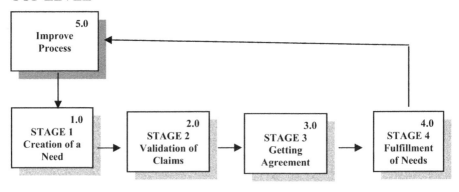

FIRST LEVEL   Here are first level flows for two of the stages.

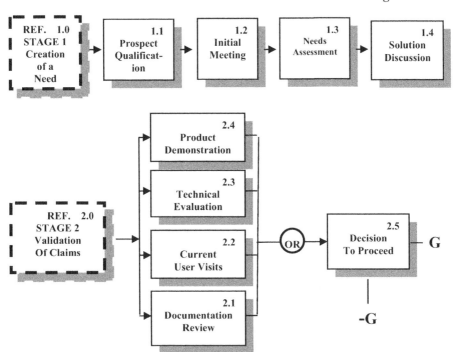

Note that the first level flow for Stage 1, *Creation of a Need,* is in a sequence that ends with a discussion with the prospect of solutions to needs identified during the *Needs Assessment* step.

Stage 2, *Validation of Claims,* exists because often prospects want access to information about the selling organization, its products and services, and customers so they can verify what it has been told by salespeople about the offering. There is no natural sequence for this stage and so the first level flow shows the steps in parallel.

Since a prospect may not choose to do all of the steps listed an OR gate is used. Also, since it is possible that the prospect may choose not to proceed with consideration of the offering after going through one or more of the steps, GO-NO GO paths are indicated. Second level flows for each of the first level steps exist and are covered in my book: *Integrated Sales Process Management, A methodology for improving sales effectiveness in the 21st Century,* available from the publisher, Author House at www.authorhouse.com.

The steps in defining the work effort are:

1. Divide project work into phases. The top level of an FFBD should fulfill this step.
2. Create first level flows.
3. If necessary, create lower level flows for each block in the first level flow.
4. Define "products" or "deliverables" from each lower level block.
5. Identify specific work steps to create the deliverables. Reiterate. (See the deliverables/work step format below.)
6. Group work steps into tasks, if they already aren't at a task level.
7. Define logical relationships among deliverables and tasks. That is, indicate which steps have to be done in a given sequence and which tasks can be done in parallel. Reiterate

Defining the deliverables and identifying work steps to create them

This addresses steps 4 and 5 (above) in defining the work effort.

> **Success comes from outputs, not from activity.**

Deliverables are the things created by project work

Three keys to deliverable definition are;

- That all important deliverables are defined
- That the definitions are clear and unambiguous
- That they are documented

Deliverable categories

- Development-related (e.g. test plans)   ⎱ Purpose of the
- Management-related (e.g. project plans) ⎰ deliverable
- Marketing-related
- Draft   ⎱ State of the
                                           ⎰ deliverable

- Final
- Tangible (e.g. documents)   ⎱ Physical form
- Intangible (e.g. events)
- Internal
- Communicable   ⎱ Intended
                                           ⎰ audience
- User

Some comments regarding deliverables and work steps

- For each lower level function, list all deliverables of each category that come to mind (above).
- Some document deliverables are done in two steps, draft form followed by final form. Be sure to list both.
- Some types of deliverables are produced more than once, e.g. monthly project status reports. Determine how many times each is needed.
- Determine previous deliverables that are inputs to a given deliverable and determine which downstream deliverables/tasks will require the completion of the deliverable. This is how you determine the precedence relationships among tasks.
- Some deliverables are associated with communications with users, management, vendors, technical people, etc. Be sure to be specific about these.

Example of defining deliverables and associated work steps

Suppose one of the work elements in a project was to define the user requirements for an integrated sales management system. Suppose there are several organizations and people that must be contacted. Here is a format you might use for deliverables and associated work steps for interview activities:

Deliverable and Work Step List	
Phase: User requirements definition	**Project:** ISM Implementation
Deliverables	**Work Steps**
Interview appointments	*Set up interviews*
Interview guides	*Prepare interview guides*
Interview notes	*Conduct interviews/take notes*
Summary of interviews	*Summarize findings from interviews*
	Travel to/from interviews

Criteria for combining work steps into tasks (Step 6 in defining the work effort)

- *Size.* Small tasks support accurate estimating. (6 to 40 labor hours is a good size)
- *Consistency.* Deals with similarity of function within a task. Deliverables are related or support one another.
- *Assignability.* Refers to the combination of size and consistency. A goal is to assign one (at most 2) people to most tasks.

- *Define deliverables.* Tasks exist only to create deliverables. There must be at least one deliverable per task.
- *Loss of control situations.* Creating physical products puts control with the project team.
- *Expressive verbs.* Each activity (within a task) should start with a strong action verb, such as *write, evaluate,* or *consult.* Avoid weak verbs such as *do, make, get,* or *finish.*

Planning Step 3.0: Estimating the Work Effort

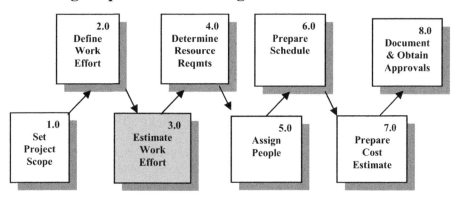

Work effort estimating is a complex process involving many factors and their interactions. So many variables are involved that it is intellectually difficult to handle them all at one time. So we use **2-stage estimating**. This reduces complexity by considering groups of factors separately and it helps estimators focus on the nature of the work itself, the performer and the environmental factors. It also improves documentation. It works like this:

- *Stage 1:* A specific, often unrealistic, set of personal and environmental assumptions is made. Against this backdrop, an intermediate estimate (called the *par* estimate) that takes work complexity variables into account is prepared.
- *Stage 2:* The original assumptions are relaxed and the par work effort estimate is adjusted to account for the now assumed performers and environment. This complete estimate is used for later planning steps and for project control.

There are five basic inputs to the estimating process:
1. The task definitions (from Planning Step 2.0). The nature of the deliverables affects labor talents that are needed. Clear statements help.

36

2. Assumptions. Guesses about the future. Includes constraints. Must be documented.

3. The people needed. How many, what knowledge and skills.

4. The project environment. Surrounding realities that affect performance, such as work locations, number of organizations to deal with and so forth. More on this later.

5. Experience from prior projects, including actual labor hours from comparable projects.

This figure illustrates the steps in estimating the work effort (labor hours per task) and where and how the basic inputs are used:

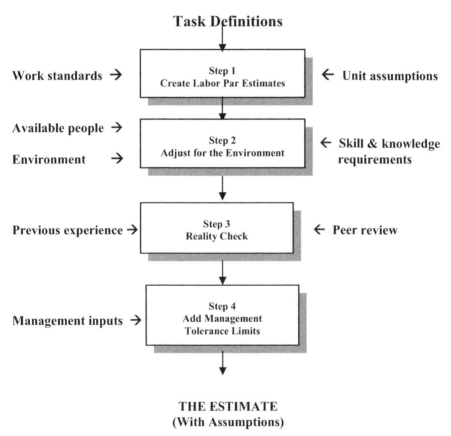

Task Definitions

Work standards → | Step 1 Create Labor Par Estimates | ← Unit assumptions

Available people →
Environment → | Step 2 Adjust for the Environment | ← Skill & knowledge requirements

Previous experience → | Step 3 Reality Check | ← Peer review

Management inputs → | Step 4 Add Management Tolerance Limits |

THE ESTIMATE
(With Assumptions)

The Work Effort Estimating Steps

Each step is discussed below.

Work Effort Estimating Step 1: Create the Labor Par Estimate.

A par estimate assumes that the task will be performed
- By a single individual
- Of average experience
- Working at least 90% of his/her time on the project, and
- Where there is no more than one user to have interactions with during the task.

A par estimate also assumes that the system involved is not overly complex, that no new techniques are being employed, and other factors.

As this step is carried out, the assumptions made about these issues should be documented

---

Work Effort Estimation

Task: Interview Sales Managers

Objective: Determine system requirements of the sales managers

Task Steps	Unit Name	No. of Units	Hours/ Unit	Par Hours
1. Set up interviews	interview	3	$1/4$	$3/4$
2. Prepare interview guides	Interview	1	3	3
3. Travel to/from interviews	interview	3	2	6
4. Conduct interviews	Interview	3	3	9
5. Summarize findings	Interview	3	2	6

Total Par Estimate   24 $3/4$

====================

STEP 1. **Work step & deliverable estimate**
     Determine number of units
          Estimate hours per unit
               Extend to get hours per step
                    Sum for total par hours for task

Work Effort Estimating Step 2: Adjust Par Estimate for the Environment

The set of factors shown in the following table are taken from a project management methodology for information systems development. They are a method for explicitly dealing with common assumptions in a two-stage estimating process, as we are employing here.

The planner should focus on the meaning of the factors rather than the specific weights used. A given project is likely to have several unique adjustment factors in addition to the common set. The key here is that it is very important to consider each actual or assumed factor explicitly and individually.

Table of Adjustment Factors		
Team Size	**Average Team Experience**	**No. Orgs. To Coordinate**
One -0.1	All senior -0.1	One 0 Par
Two 0 Par	Mostly senior 0 Par	Two 0.1
3 or 4 0.1	½ senior 0.1	3 or 4 0.2
5 to 7 0.2	Mostly junior 0.2	Over 4 0.4
Over 7 0.3	All junior 0.4	
% Time on other work	**Project Manager Experience**	**User Support**
0-10% 0 Par	3+ prior projects 0 Par	Strong sponsor -0.1
10-30% 0.1	1-2 prior projects 0.1	Average 0 Par
30-50% 0.2	No prior projects 0.2	Hard to reach 0.1
Over 50% 0.3	None + new 0.3	Remote 0.2
Project Size	**Project length**	**Experience as a Team**
Small & medium 0 Par	Under 1 year 0 Par	Often work together 0 Par
Large 0.1	1-2 years 0.1	Some work together 0.1
Super 0.2	Over 2 years 0.3	Strangers 0.2
Program Complexity	**System Complexity**	**File Complexity**
Very simple -0.1	Very simple -0.1	Very simple -0.1
Average 0 Par	Average 0 Par	Average 0 Par
Complex 0.1	Complex 0.1	Complex 0.1
Very complex 0.2	Very complex 0.2	Very complex 0.2
Project Mgr. Continuity		
After the change 0.3		

Such a form can be used to document original project assumptions. All you need do is place an arrow (➔) to indicate the assumption for each factor.

Not all of these factors are meaningful for marketing projects. They are provided for completeness.

Simple Example:		**Case 1**		**Case 2**
Par estimate		100 hours		100 hours
Average team experience	Junior	0.4	Senior	-0.1
% time on other work	50%	0.2	25%	0.1
Total adjustments		0.6		0.0
Additions due to adjustments		60 hours		0 hours
Adjusted task estimate		**160 hours**		**100 hours**

Above is a simple example of the use of the factors in the table. We use only two of the factors:

- Average team experience
- Percent of time on other work

In the following example, based on the par estimate for the "interview sales managers" task, another factor not covered in the table is added to show that there can be other environmental factors that impact the labor content of tasks.

Let's review the arithmetic in arriving at a total estimate of 42 hours. First of all, 42 hours is a rounding of 42.05 hours = 24.75+3.8+6+7.5.

In coming up with the 3.8 adjustment for experience, we added the task step estimates for steps 1, 2, 4 and 5 ($^3/_4$+3+9+6 = 18 $^3/_4$) and rounded it to 19. Then The Table of Adjustments was consulted to get the adjustment of 0.2 to recognize the fact that John Jones experience is "junior". 0.2 x 19 = 3.8. Jones' experience was not relevant in the 6 hours of travel.

Work Effort Estimation
With Environmental Adjustments

Task: Interview Sales Managers

Objective: Determine system requirements of the sales managers

Task Steps	Unit Name	No. of Units	Hours/ Unit	Par Hours
1. Set up interviews	interview	3	1/4	3/4
2. Prepare interview guides	interview	1	3	3
3. Travel to/from interviews	interview	3	2	6
4. Conduct interviews	interview	3	3	9
5. Summarize findings	interview	3	2	6

Total Par Estimate   24 3/4

=============================

Adjustments to Par Hours:
- John Jones sales management experience is low (0.2 x 19)   3.8
- One interview will require travel out of Dallas area   6
- John Jones is available only 1/2 time   (0.3 x 24 3/4)   7.5

Total hours with environmental adjustments   42

Next we address the half-time availability. Then *The Table of Adjustments* was consulted to get the adjustment of 0.3 for the fact that John Jones is spending 50% of his time on other work   0.3 x 24¾ = 7.425 which is rounded to 7.5.

This may seem a little confusing at first, but it works.

Work Effort Estimating Step 3: Do a Reality Check

This is the step in work effort estimating where we apply previous experience. Look at the adjusted hours and ask: "How reasonable are these estimates?" Are they too high? Or are they too low? If you have maintained a history of the actual labor expended on projects by project type, compare the estimates with previous similar projects. Don't use this step to give into pressures for a *small* estimate.

Other Reality testing methods that could be employed are:
- A second look. Making the estimates again.
- Employ two or more estimating methods.
- Have someone else make estimates using the same method as you have used.
- Have your estimates reviewed by a peer group.
- Have a group of people make the estimates and achieve a consensus on them.

Work Effort Estimating Step 4: Add Management Tolerance Limits

Management, of course, does not give blank checks to project teams. There may be policies that need to be taken into consideration. If these policies include maximum funding levels there may be no need to check with them if the estimates are within the policy range.

The Role of Assumptions in Work Effort Estimating

The four estimating steps lead to the estimate for the work effort. It should include:
- The labor hours per activity being estimated. This may be only the activities for a given project phase. See the discussion on *Using Phase-Limited Planning* below.
- The skill and knowledge requirements by activity.
- Allocation of activities to various responsible groups, such as users and customers.
- Documentation on the assumptions considered in the estimating.

There are four categories of assumptions that can be considered:
- *Project-related.* These are tied to project objectives, work methods and so forth. Examples are team size and composition and volatility of the requirements.

42

- *Customer-related.* These are tied to the structure, operating methods, etc. of the customer. Examples are management processes used by the customer, the availability of customer resources, and the quality of the customer's documentation.
- *Environmental.* These are tied to the project's surrounding environment. Examples are physical location, time of year, organizational complexity and availability of support.
- *Work situation.* These are tied to team interaction with other projects and processes. Examples are contention for resources, level of participation, delays and waiting times.

Reasons for documenting assumptions. We document assumptions because:

- unwritten assumptions are forgotten,
- there is a tendency to twist assumptions to make things come out right,
- there is less of a chance of misunderstanding the work,
- the estimates are more *saleable* to higher levels, and
- the assumptions provide a basis for revising plans as reality replaces assumptions.

The idea is to write down what you are thinking when you make an estimate.

Factors that make work effort estimating difficult

- Uncertainty and unpredictability of future events or conditions, such as the number of interviews needed, availability of resources when you need them.
- Lack of adequate data so that you have to make assumptions.
- Sensitivity to assumptions.
- Lack of estimating technology such as guidelines and procedures.
- Use of customer personnel and your lack of control over them.
- Selling pressures.

Problems you may have if you don't have individual activity estimates

- Assignments are not clear.
- Scheduling is more difficult because you can't determine task durations.
- Harder to control schedule and cost.
- Harder to *sell* the estimate and plan. Bulk estimates are subject to anybody's guess.

Estimating Principles:

- Better estimates come from:
  - ➢ Knowing the work to be done
  - ➢ Bite-sized work elements
  - ➢ Explicit treatment of environmental factors
  - ➢ Applying past experience
- Forward visibility is limited
- Have courage to tell the truth, at least to ourselves
- Give notice of changes as soon as possible

Networking -- Dealing with relationships among work effort elements

Work effort definition is not complete until the ways that the elements of work are related to one another is documented. Some tasks can't be started until other tasks have been completed. Such tasks are called *dependent.*

If we have two activities and either activity may be performed first or they may be performed at the same time, they are said to be *parallel* with one another.

A *network* shows the string of relations among a number of tasks that can include dependent and parallel tasks.

Networks improve insight, help make the project schedule realistic, (as we shall see below) improve communication and help establish progress control.

Mechanics of Networking

The vocabulary of networking is simple. There are three elements:

- ▪ *Activities.* These are modules of work effort identified by Activity name, Activity number, and Starting and Ending numbers. Activity name or number is written above or below the line.
- ▪ *Events.* These are logical delimiters for activities. Events are represented by circles at the beginning and end of an activity and are numbered.

Event Activity **Event**

60 70

- *Dummy activities.* These are used to portray a dependency where there is no real activity to connect two events. They are represented by a dashed arrow.

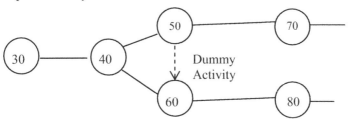

Network Rules and Conventions

- Length of lines do not denote duration
- Network must have one start event and a *unique* end event
- All activity and event numbers must be unique
- Only one *real* activity (solid line) should terminate at an event
- There must be only one *real* activity terminating at each event
- Networks illustrate logic of work, not resource constraints
- No double-headed arrows for dummy activities
- Avoid backward flows
- Avoid crossing lines.

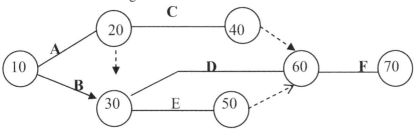

Steps in Network Construction

1. Prepare a list of activities and deliverables.
2. Identify immediate dependents/predecessors for each activity
3. Draw the network
4. Reality test the logic of the network
5. Redraft physical network to improve accuracy and clarity.

Planning Step 4.0: Determining Resource Requirements

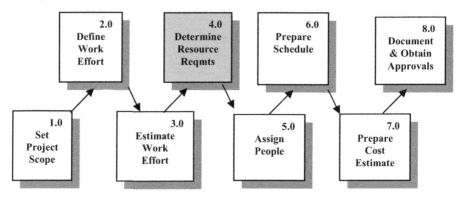

Here are the major resource categories required on projects.

- *People.* (By numbers and capabilities)
  - o Project team members
  - o Other company resources
  - o Customer personnel
  - o Vendors
- *Technology.* Examples are:
  - o Methodologies
  - o Standards
  - o Computers
  - o Simulation tools
- *Support services.* Examples are:
  - o Document preparation
  - o Reproduction services
  - o Technical editing
  - o Administrative services
- *Information.* Examples are:
  - o Statistical information
  - o Status of company products and services
  - o Financial models and decision criteria of customers
  - o Information on competitors' offerings
- *Facilities and equipment.* Examples are:
  - o Office space and furniture
  - o Communications facilities
  - o Supplies (such as calculators and forms)

Resource requirements statements are used for:
- Input into assigning the right capability to the right task
- Input into cost estimation. You can't set realistic budgeting without complete knowledge of the resource requirements.
- Obtaining company approvals. Some resource categories (e.g. capital investments and outside services) require special approvals.
- Determining how much resource is needed from customers.
- Input into project organizing. We can negotiate better with resource suppliers when we know exactly what we need.
- Resource control criteria. When you specify what you want explicitly, you can more easily manage whether you got the quality and quantity you specified.

Planning Step 5.0: Assigning People to the Tasks

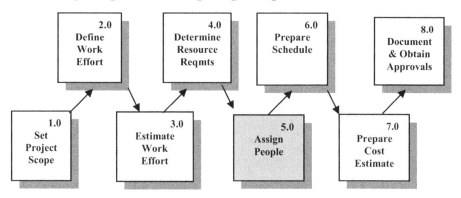

You must first determine the availability of people that you may want to assign to the projects. Here is an availability work sheet format that has been used successfully by the author.

Project Availability Worksheet										
For: J. Smith						**Project:** ISM System				
Month: January 2004										
Dates →	1	2	5	6	7	8	9	...	29	30
Time Unavailable								...		
Holidays	8							.....		
Vacation								.....		
Training		3	3					.....		
Other projects								.....		
Other		1	1	2	2	2	2	.....	2	2
TOTAL	8	4	4	2	2	2	2	.....	2	2
Available Time for Project	0	4	4	6	6	6	6	.....	6	6

Planning Step 6.0: Preparing the Project Schedule

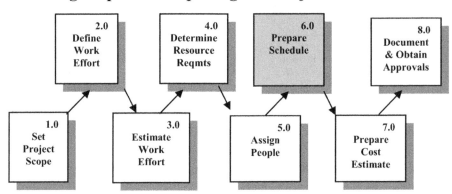

Management is often more concerned with system availability than how much it costs. Therefore the development of attainable and believable schedules is extremely important. The key to detailed scheduling is being realistic about the amount of elapsed time each task will take. The key inputs to this are recognizing the impact of multiple people on a task, the average productivity for the staff and delays such as service turn-around times.

The role of scheduling is to:
- set realistic expectatione about how long the project will take,
- allow enough time to *do it right the first time,*

- forecast when resources are needed, and
- indicate what is the best time for the training that will be needed

Feasible schedules come from:

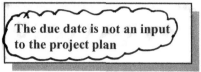

- Knowing people availability, both inside and outside the organization
- Realistic work effort (labor hour) estimates
- Having people full time.
- Not scheduling people 100% of their time
- Using one person to one task (where possible)
- Not changing the schedule to please the user
- Not *imposing* due dates. Due dates are the result of balancing the scope of the system, the resources to be applied to the project and the quality controls that will be in place.

Project Schedule Preparation Steps

Here are the 5 steps to be followed in creating the project schedule. The information flow demands that they be done in order.

| Step 1 Calculate Task Durations | → | Step 2 Determine Resource Availability | → | Step 3 Create 1st Cut Network Schedule | → | Step 4 Prepare Resource Loading Chart | → | Step 5 Optimize the Schedule |

Schedule Preparation Step 1: Calculating Task Durations

To prepare a project schedule you first have to calculate realistic durations for each of the tasks. In

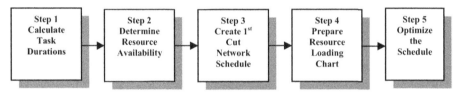

There's never enough time to do it right ---- but there's always time to do it over.
                              Heskimen's Law

this step we apply factors that only affect elapsed time, factors such as service delays, people availability and loading, etc. Step 1 is too often omitted or mishandled. Several kinds of information are required, as depicted below on *Figure 1-D: Inputs to Duration Calculation*. The accuracy of task duration calculations is susceptible to errors or omissions in any of them.

49

Work effort estimates, as we have seen earlier, are stated in terms of man-hours, or perhaps man-days. A question might be: *Why can't we just use that for the duration?* There are many reasons why not.

Here are a few that are related to the initial assignments to tasks:
- Different people work at different paces
- The assigned person may be available for the project only part-time.
- More than one person may be assigned
- Holidays and vacations may intervene
- Other projects may be competing for the same resources
- Dates when customer decision meetings are held may fall at inconvenient times
- Standard service turn-around times.

Initial assignments give the information on what person or people are assigned to the task, what percent of the time they are available, what their days of unavailability are, and when will they be available.

There are several types of *assumptions and constraints* that are important to duration calculations and do not directly affect other planning steps.

One of these assumptions is personnel who could be available and their assumed talents

Another assumption is the number of hours in a *productive day*. Productive day hours are almost always fewer than standard work day hours of, say, 8 hours. This assumption is to account for time lost that is hard to keep track of, even after the fact. Examples are coffee breaks, bathroom time, unexpected telephone calls or meetings, administrative duties, late lunches, and so on.

The planner applies these two types of assumptions to the work effort estimate and calculates a *base duration* for the task

Loading factors that allow for time lost that you can account for, at least after the fact, modify the base duration. These include:
- *Non-project time* such as holidays, vacations, sick leave, jury duty, and training
- *Contention,* such as work on other projects or the line job of the individual. This explains why a person is available only part time.
- *Nature of work time* which accounts for such things as waiting time for services such as graphics, word processing and computer processing, approval cycle length (e.g. from company management

and customers), delayed meetings and reschedules, travel time, external information delays, external rework (e.g. corrections of errors and omissions by others) and management interferences

Some potential sources of *constraints* are:
- Customer requirements (e.g. due dates for drafts, final reports and other documents)
- Company management requirements (e.g. specific review of deliverables)
- Policy statements (e.g. no overtime for clerical people)
- Procedural (e.g. legal must approve all agreements and contracts)
- Product availability

When faced with constraints in scheduling, you must accommodate to them or get them relaxed.

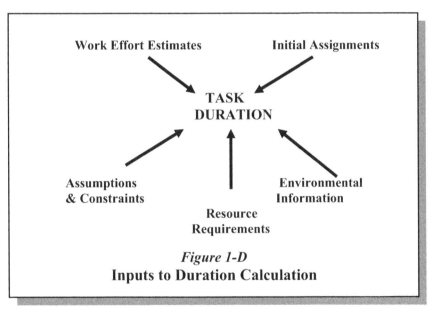

Figure 1-D
Inputs to Duration Calculation

Resource requirements inputs were discussed above, under *Planning Step 4.0*.

Environmental information used in duration calculations, and in scheduling in general, include
- Location of customer people and facilities
- Dates when customer decision meetings are held
- Other company projects competing for the same resources
- Internal document approval process

51

Example of a Duration Calculation

TASK DURATION ESTIMATE

Task: Interview Sales Managers (1 person assigned)

Adjusted Work Effort Estimate	**42 Hours**
(**Productive work day** = 6 hours)	
Base Duration (Divide by Productive work day) 42/6 =	**7 Days**
Non-Project Time assumptions * 10 %	0.7 **Days**
Sub-total	7.7 **Days**
Contention (Available ½ time)	+ 7.7 **Days**
Nature of Work:	
Delayed meetings /reschedules	+ 1.0 **Days**
Typing and reproduction of findings	+ 1.0 **Days**
TOTAL	17.4 **Days**

Task Duration (some rounding) 17 ½ **Days**

* Actual effects of holidays, vacations and sick time are reflected when putting the durations on a time scale – i.e. when you find out where the task falls.

Schedule Preparation Step 2: Determine Resource Availability

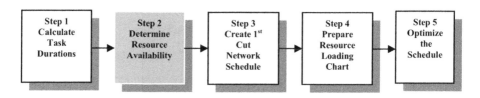

Step 1 Calculate Task Durations	Step 2 Determine Resource Availability	Step 3 Create 1st Cut Network Schedule	Step 4 Prepare Resource Loading Chart	Step 5 Optimize the Schedule

This is the step where we confirm the timing of availability of the project team members and other resources. (See **Planning Step 4.0**, earlier, for a list of resource categories and types.)

Schedule Preparation Step 3: Creating a First-Cut Network Schedule

This is done by building the network of activities and events, using the task durations for the lengths of the activities, and timing out this network.

This provides great visibility of the work effort. From it the critical path, i.e. the shortest path to completion of the project, emerges. All of the dependencies are exposed.

Here are some network scheduling terms we will use:

Path: Any connected sequence of activities, including dummy activities, that goes from the initial network event to the final event.
Critical path: Any path along which slippage in any activity will cause an equal amount of slippage in the entire project.
Slack: Amount by which an activity may slip without affecting the project completion date. Slack is applied only to activities that are not on the critical path.
Earliest completion date (ECD): Earliest date that an activity can finish, given upstream structure and activity durations.
Network value: Total elapsed time required to complete the network. This is synonymous with the length of the critical path.
Latest start date (LSD): Latest date on which an activity may start without compromising an already determined project completion date.
Earliest start date (ESD): Earliest possible date to start an activity, given upstream network structure.

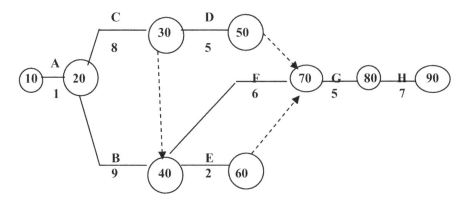

53

Michael W. Lodato Ph. D.

Timing out the network We now go through the steps to determine the critical path for the network. We assume that this network represents the tasks for a given phase of a project.

Here is the notation we will use so that you get all scheduling information on one graphic.

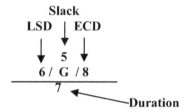

The steps to timing the network are:
1. Calculate the ECDs for all activities including dummy activities. Calculate from left to right, adding the duration to the largest ECD of the activity's predecessors.
2. Calculate the LSDs for all activities, including dummy activities. Calculate from right to left, subtracting the duration from the smallest LSD of the dependent activities
3. Find the critical path by working from right to left, matching the LSD of dependent activities to the ECD of a predecessor. The length, (duration), of the critical path is the network value – the total elapsed time to complete the network.
4. Calculate slack. Slack = LSD + Duration – ECD. As you would expect, all the activities on the critical path (bold line on the graphic) have 0 slack

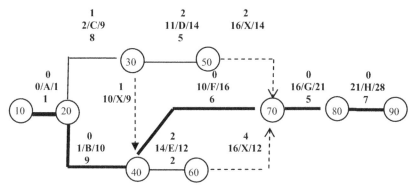

Schedule Preparation Step 4: Prepare the Resource Loading Chart

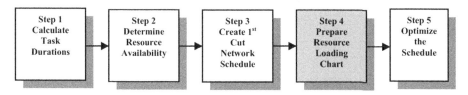

A resource-loading chart is a technique for displaying resource usage information organized to show the workload on each person or other resource. The project management tool presented here is called *Bar Charting*.

A *bar chart* shows units of work effort (activities, tasks) laid out against a time scale. The bars that represent the activities span the planned start and complete dates for them. Bar charts are useful for many purposes including scheduling, communication, status assessment, and project progress control. They are simple and familiar.

A Basic Bar Chart

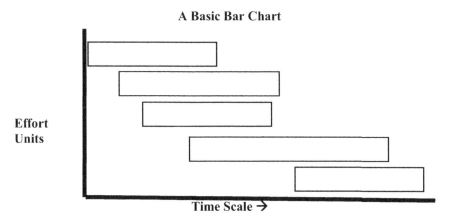

The time scale is on the horizontal axis. The scale can be fine or coarse. The work effort units are listed down the vertical axis. Work effort units can be at different levels. That is, a bar can represent:

- An activity
- A phase
- The whole project

The bars illustrate the span of time of each activity. The left edge is the start date; the right edge is the end date. As we shall see, additional information can be added, such as vacations and holidays.

Adding more information to a bar

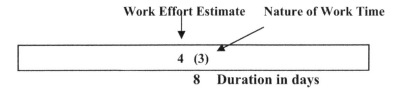

Remember that *nature of work (n.o.w) time* accounts for such things as waiting time for services, approval cycle length, delayed meetings and reschedules, travel, external work and management interferences. Some of this time is recoverable by having people assigned to the task work on other tasks. However, some *nature of work time*, such as contention time, is not recoverable.

Here is an example of a resource-loading chart. The left edge of each bar is set at the *Earliest Start Date (ESD)*. The numbers on the right of each bar give the task durations, so you don't have to depend upon "eye-balling". Durations could include contention time.

Resource Loading Chart

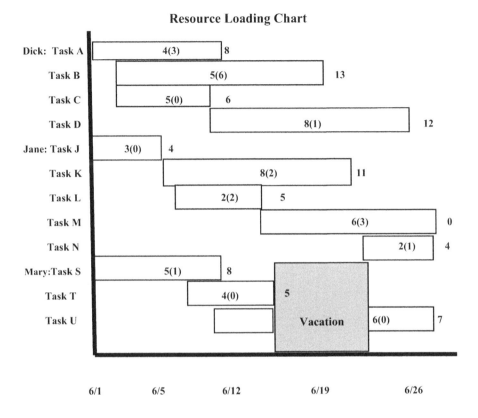

Note that Dick has 39 days of work durations over a 20-day period. Ten days are recoverable *nature of work* time. The real conflict is 9 days.

Non-project time, such as Mary's vacation and perhaps training time can be shown. Bars may be broken to show *non-project time.*

Another level of analysis is needed.
- Some recoverable n.o.w. time may be unusable if there are no parallel activities.
- You can't move tasks to the left because of earliest start dates (ESD)
- You need to know the substance of the n.o.w. time.
- For example, the one day of n.o.w. time on Task S may be used only on Task T, and only if it falls in the last 3 days of the task. See the overlap between Tasks S and T.
- Sometimes tasks are swapped to avoid wasting n.o.w. time.

We now add additional information to the Resource Loading Chart.
- You can use vertical dashed lines to show Latest Completion Dates (LCD), taken from the network. The distance from the bar to the dashed line is the slack for the activity.
- Slack shows how far we can move the task to the right without delaying the project. This is useful in schedule optimization.
- The graphic technique integrates network data with the bar chart.

Resource Loading Chart

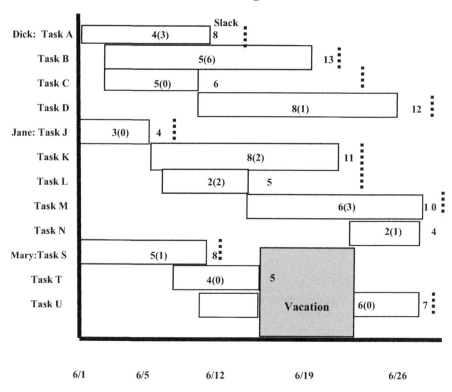

This depiction is useful
- It reveals potential conflict resolutions
- We can move an entire task to the right or extend the duration (by the amount of slack).
- But don't use up all of the slack; otherwise you won't be able to weather future problems. A project usually has several critical paths.

- Extensions of a task must match resource availability. For example, 3 days of Task U's slack fall during Mary's vacation.
- We can also show when task deliverables are produced. (See arrows, ▲, on the chart)

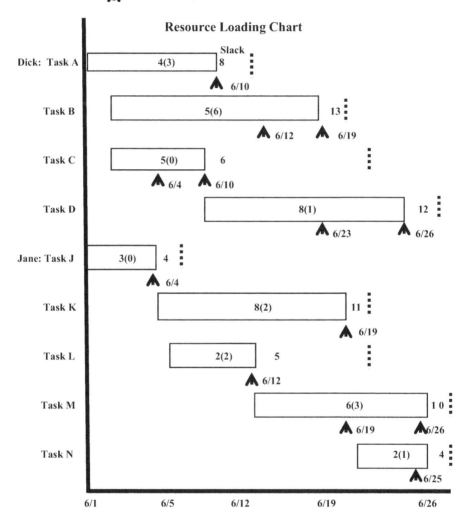

Resource Loading Chart

Some tips in using resource-loading charts:
- Group each person's activities together
- Activities assigned to more than one person appear in each person's section.
- List tasks in chronological order.

- Use a fine time scale to show small activities and use large-format paper.
- Use pencil. To err is human.

Schedule Preparation Step 5: Optimize the Schedule

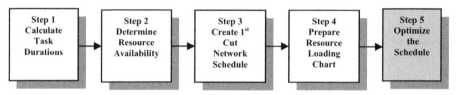

This step is an iteration process through the first 4 steps until you get a workable schedule.

In optimizing the schedule we use three criteria, usually iteratively (several passes needed):

- Acceptability
  - o Are we working people too hard?
  - o Are completion dates for the project and key milestones consistent with objectives, constraints and commitments?
- Attainability
  - o Do we have the resources to meet the schedule?
  - o Are our assumptions realistic?
  - o Have we been too optimistic about turnarounds for support and decisions?
  - o Are the workloads reasonable?
- Manageable risk (There should be some risk)
  - o Are the risks of failure too high?
  - o Have we built resiliency into the plan to absorb future unseen problems?
  - o Have we allowed time for re-work?

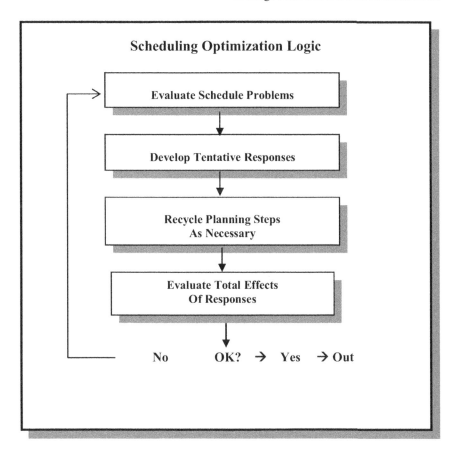

Evaluate Schedule Problems

The network structure and calculations and the resource loading charts facilitate the identification of schedule problems because you can see everything in relationship to other things. It is important that we deal with specific issues, not general ones. For example:

- o What happens if the customer is late in supplying the data?
- o Is Mary's workload consistent with the fact that she is available only 25% of her time?

Develop Tentative Responses

Here we create alternative solutions to schedule problems. There are three types of optimizing responses to be considered:

- • Costless internal solutions, such as:

- o Reapplying *Nature of Work* time
- o Using up activity slack days
- o Reassigning activities within the existing team
- o Extending the completion date for a phase or the project.
- o Decomposing activities to increase parallelism.
- Costless external solutions, such as:
  - o Obtaining more capable people
  - o Reducing the project scope
  - o Reducing service and decision turnaround times
- Increased-cost solutions, such as:
  - o Adding people to the project team
  - o Obtaining outside support
  - o Procuring technology

Usually, combinations of responses are used.

Recycle Planning Steps, As Necessary

Here we play *what if* games.
- What if we revise the work effort estimates?
- What if we drop some of the tasks all together? (Although this may cause more rework later.)
- What if we add people?.

Evaluate Total Affects of Responses

Some solutions may be ineffective. For example, experience shows that adding people to a late project, unless it is done very carefully, usually makes it later.

A solution to a given problem may cause other problems. For example, solving an overload in one month may create one in another month.

The optimization process should be iterated until:
- All significant problems are removed.
- Only manageable problems remain
- You know you must change project objectives or constraints.

Scheduling Outputs

Project scheduling yields several outputs. Some are new information elements and others are revisions to earlier planning decisions. Here are some;

- **A list of activity start and completion dates**. This is the central output of scheduling.
- **Milestone dates for management consumption.** These include end of phase dates and key decision dates.
- **Revisions to earlier planning products.** These could include change of scope, change in deliverables and/or tasks, change in work effort estimates, change in resource requirements, change in assignments.
- **Final project network.** The network structure may be changed and/or information could be added regarding durations, critical path, slack times, and so forth.
- **Optimized resource-loading charts.**
- **Scheduling Assumptions.** This is a very important communication vehicle that substantiates the other outputs

Planning Step 7.0: Preparing the Cost Estimate

This is the step where we summarize the results of the previous steps in financial terms by producing reports that provides cost estimates for labor, computer use, outside support, and other resources. See *Project Plan* example, below, to visualize how the cost information can be summarized.

Planning Step 8.0: Documenting the Plan and Gaining Approval

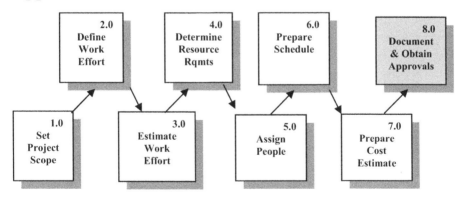

The next few pages give illustrations of some project plan documents.

Project Task Assignments

For: J. Smith Project: ISM System

Month: January 2004

TASK	ADJ. HRS.	1	2	5	6	7	8	9	....	29	30
Dates →											
Hours/Day Available for Project		0	4	4	6	6	6	6	....	6	6
		H							....		
2.2.2 Review current System	10	O L I	4	4	2				....		
2.2.3 Generate User Requirements	18	D A Y			4	6	6	2	....		
2.2.4 Consolidate User Requirements	22								4		

- Match Adjusted Hours required for tasks to the assigned person's *hours/days available for project.* (As illustrated)
- Use pencil because of schedule adjustments due to interdependencies
- Do this concurrently with Task Scheduling Sheet. (See below)
- The process may expose gaps of time that can be used for trivial projects, e.g. re-documenting.

Project Task Scheduling

Project: ISM System Phase: User Requirements

Month: January 2004

TASK	ASSIGNED PERSON	ADJ. HRS.	1	2	5	6	7	......	29	30
2.2.2 Review current System	J. Smith	10	H O L	4	4	2		.....		
2.2.2B	T. Jones	12	I D A	5	5	2		.....		
2.2.3 Generate User Requirements	J. Smith	18	Y			4	6	.....		
2.2.3B	T. Jones	20				5	5	.....		

- Cover the period to (whichever happens first):
  - o The next estimating milestone
  - o The end of the project
  - o The next 6 weeks
- Do this concurrently with the Task Assignment Sheet
- Use task networking charts for task interdependencies
- Put contingency tasks into the schedule (for overlooked tasks)

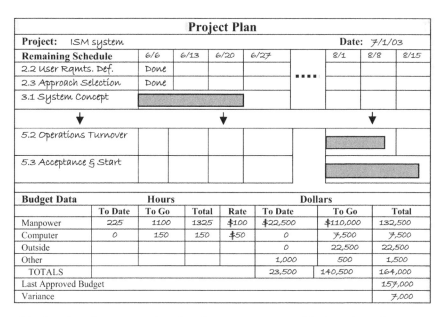

Notice that the uncompleted tasks are represented in bar chart format.

Getting the Project Plan Accepted

The chances of having the project plan accepted are enhanced when:

- The true extent of the project is visible. (It only seems *scary* at first.)
- The task/deliverable level estimates are visible
- Anticipated difficulties are accounted for explicitly.
- Annotation is provided to give further insight
- The plans appear to be *do-able* rather than overly optimistic
- You have earned credibility because you have met feasible plans.

Using Phase-Limited Planning – Re-plan at Key Milestones

The effort to define, estimate, staff and schedule the project work elements can sometimes be considerable. Besides, you just don't have a clear enough visibility on later phases until you have performed on earlier phases. As you complete a phase you have a better picture on:

- where you are,
- what is left to be done,
- what resources will be available for the up-coming phase
- how the team is performing,
- how the environmental factors are working out, and so forth.

Therefore the recommendation is to do such detailed task definitions phase-by-phase with the planning for subsequent phases done at a summary level, as implied by the following two graphics.

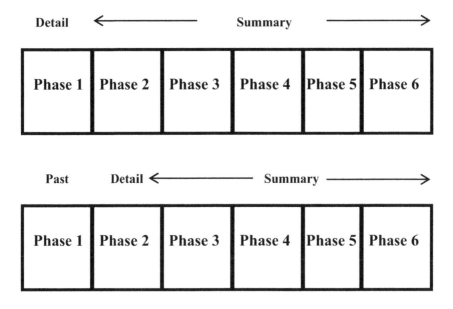

5. Project Execution Process

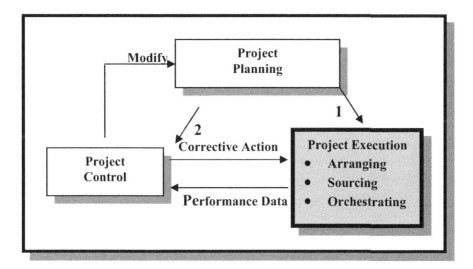

1 indicates that project planning specifies the project activities.
2 indicates that project planning specifies the control activities and the control criteria.

Arranging

In this management activity, the project manager decides on the proper organization and relationship of resources and processes to implement the project plan and, in so doing, most effectively and efficiently achieve the desired results and outcomes – the project objectives. The concern is to set up the elements of the project – people, resources, tasks, procedures and other processes – and relate them to one another.

Here are some points to consider in arranging.

Creating a Proper Environment for Successful Projects

- Have sound policies
- Avoid imposed deadlines
- Give users responsibility for solving the business problem
- Provide adequate administrative resources
- Have documentation and other standards

Documentation Standards

Proper documentation improves communications and reduces personnel costs. For example, documentation at the end of each phase helps users determine whether the right problems are being addressed, what the alternatives are and if there will be an adequate return on investment. Good documentation protects the investment in the new system, product launch, or other major project result. These results often change and they contain errors that must be corrected.

The following comments speak to the value of the timely creation of good documentation

- Complete documentation standards, especially if accompanied by good guidelines; assure that the documentation meets an acceptable level of quality.
- Forms accompanied by instructions for their completion and examples saves valuable time, assures pertinent data is included, and discourages verbosity.
- Project workbooks and files provide an orderly mechanism for handling the documentation during the project.
- Event-driven documentation reviews assure that the documentation is produced at the proper time, is of acceptable quality, and is formally accepted by those who subsequently use it. Postponement of documentation completion, while it temporarily reduces project costs, maximizes confusion, waste and duplication of effort.

The question arises: *How much documentation is enough?*

The answer is that you have enough when a reasonably intelligent person, not familiar with the system, new product launch or other major project result, can acquire sufficient knowledge for his or her purposes through reading the documentation. *Enough* is a qualitative assessment of information – not a numerical count of pages. So when creating documentation one should be guided by

- How complicated the launch, program, system or other major result is
- How technically sophisticated the primary users are
- How many people are involved in the project
- How long the program will be implemented or the system will be used
- How frequently the requirements will change.

The documentation standards should call for the creation of a document at the end of each phase. This document is a synthesis of the results of the phase tasks that are relevant to the intended readers

Documentation guidelines suggest what should be written and why it should be included. When checklists and forms are used, complete instructions should be given (perhaps on the back of the form) covering when it should be used, what it is to be used for and how to complete it. Sometimes an example of a completed form (as found in this book) will shorten the time taken to complete it.

Ingredients of a Good Project

- Project manager
- Project organization
- Project administration
- System plan
- Project plan
- Project reviews
- Management support
- Proper phasing

The Project Organization

A key component of the arranging activity is the establishment of the project organization.

The elements of organizing include project structure, communication, acquisition of resources and procedures. This is where the key players on the project, the roles that they play, the relationships they have with one another and other organizational issues are addressed.

You want to set up an organization that assures and facilitates participation by management and enough other suitable resources and you want to assure that the project has enough priority so that the suitable resources will be made available.

Some of the steps in setting up the organization are:
- Select the *Project Manager* – the person who has overall responsibility for the project
- Select the *User Coordinator* – whose function is to facilitate the project manager's access to information and people in the user organization.
- Set up coordination with the *Project Administrator* (See below).

- Set up the *Steering Committee* and get commitments from committee members.
- Identify task-doer resources for assignment to the tasks.
- Prepare the Project Organization Memorandum

What a Project Manager Does
- Gives credit where credit is due
- Conducts periodic reviews
- Challenges the team members through assignments
- Keeps the team informed
- Applies pressure selectively
- Remind everyone that it is a team effort

The Project Administrator

Methodologies work only to the degree that resources are applied to their administration. This is true whether it is a project management methodology or an integrated selling process. Someone has to be accountable and do the administration for the documentation of the project plans, task descriptions, forms and checklists, the setting up of meetings, and so forth. It is strongly suggested that someone be appointed as the *Project Administrator (PA)*. The *PA* is someone who serves all projects – not just the one under discussion. As lessons are learned on earlier projects, the *PA* updates the methodology so that what is learned is not lost to the organization.

For example, there may be improvements to the project planning process and the forms and checklists that are used. The *PA* should be responsible to see that new and modified forms are designed, approved, produced in sufficient number and distributed. He/she should also see that training on the improvements is designed and given.

It may also be discovered that the *Project Repository* (See below, under Orchestrating) could benefit from some additional structure. That being the case, the *PA* should gather recommendations, document the structure and produce packages.

As projects are carried out, project members will undoubtedly deviate from the task descriptions, employ new forms and checklists, or make changes to existing ones. You want to encourage everyone to make recommendations. Then the *PA* can get the improvements documented, printed and distributed.

Project Monitoring
- Steering committee (to whom project commitments are made)

- Project manager (who makes commitment for project performance)
- User representative (who makes commitments for the user and provides support on the project)

Potential Pitfalls for Project Managers

- Planning based on faulty assumptions
- Vital reporting functions missing
- Inability to encourage motivation
- Unwelcome and unnecessary involvement in technical areas

Sourcing

Sourcing is the management activity of locating and obtaining all the resources needed for the project.

Here are the major resource categories required on projects.

• *People*. (By numbers and capabilities)
  Project team members & other company resources
  Customer personnel & Vendors

• *Technology*
  Methodologies,
  Standards,
  Computers
  Software

• *Support services*.
  Document preparation,
  Reproduction services
  Technical editing,
  Administrative services

• *Information*
  Statistical information
  Status of company products and services
  Financial models and decision criteria of customers
  Information on competitor's offerings

• *Facilities and equipment*
  Office space and furniture,
  Supplies (e.g. calculators and forms)
  Communications facilities.

Orchestrating

It is hardly ever the case that projects go according to plan. A lot of things happen that require making adjustments. In response to this, *orchestrating* is directing, coordinating, synchronizing, and symphonizing resources in changing and dynamic environments that are often experienced in projects.

Project Execution Flow

The following graphic shows the project execution flow.

It is always a good idea for the project manager to brief the project team and any user staff directly involved in the project phase. He or she should carefully review each task description and get everyone to agree that they understand the task and their roles in them. Stress the importance of documenting information and the timely submission of status reports. The briefing would include:

- Phase objectives
- Scope of the planned work effort
- Schedules and deadlines
- Resolution of possible problems
- Roles and responsibilities of each team member
- Other pertinent issues and problems

The project manager may use the briefing to familiarize the team with tasks in the phase, answering, for example, the question: *What is the essence of the work that is to be performed in the phase*

1	2	3
Project Manager Releases Tasks	**Project Team Performs Tasks**	**Results Stored in Repository**

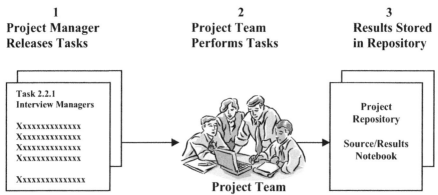

The project manager then releases a batch of tasks. The project team performs the tasks and at the completion of those tasks puts the deliverables in the Project Repository.

The Project Repository: The *Project Repository* is a very simple-minded but effective management tool. Although it can be a file cabinet, a file drawer or other repository where there are designated sections for each task, think of it as a 3-ring binder with tabs for each of the tasks that have been defined.

When tasks are released, they are taken from the tab that identifies them. When the project deliverables are completed they are placed back behind the same tab from which the task description was pulled. If the deliverable is too *large* for the binder, it is placed in the project files with a reference to its location placed behind the tab. The concept is simple, if the results are not in the project repository they are not done. Below is an example of a task description.

Time Reporting

The project staff makes a time report each week. For each assigned task they report on the time spent this week and the estimated time needed to complete the task.

The project manager tracks hours by task for control.

Weekly Time Report for Project ISM System			Week of: 4/14					
Task No.	Adjusted Hours	Assigned To	Week of:					Total
			4/7	4/14	4/21	4/28	5/5	
2.2.2	27	J. Smith	12	15	Done			27
2.2.3	30	T. Jones	4	30				30
2.2.4	36	J. Kane	30		6			36

The project manager monitors the actual vs. planned hours by phase, including "to go" hours. He/she also assesses the impact on the schedule and reports significant variances.

Michael W. Lodato Ph. D.

SAMPLE TASK DESCRIPTION
ISM IMPLEMENTATION PLAN

PROJECT: ISM Implementation

PHASE 1:   Preparation for Implementation of Integrated Sales Management System

TASK NO.: 1.10   Document sales objectives and problems to be resolved

Task Leader:

_____

TASK OBJECTIVES:
- To achieve a consensus on the problems and objectives that should be addressed by the *ISM implementation.*

DELIVERABLES:
- Problems and objectives inputs from selected groups of people.
- Summary of problems and objectives inputs.
- Consensus document of problems of concern
- Consensus document on objectives to be addressed.

STEPS:
- Prepare Potential Problems checklist and Candidate Objectives checklist
- Select group to provide inputs on problems (*Problems Group*)
- Select group to provide inputs on objectives (*Objectives Group*)
- Have *Problems Group* complete the problems checklist.
- Analyze problems inputs and prepare a summary.
- Conduct brainstorming meeting to achieve consensus on problems
- Document results.
- Have *Objectives Group* complete the objectives checklist.
- Analyze objectives inputs and prepare a summary.
- Conduct brainstorming meeting to achieve consensus on objectives
- Document results

DURATION:
- 8 days

COMMENTS:
- Consensus on problems and objectives will be used in documenting the sales and marketing plan.
- Results are important to setting the scope and nature of the *ISM* Implementation project.

Status Reporting

The project staff makes a status report each week. It consists of four parts:
1.   Task progress this week, including completions
2.   Planned completions not met together with reasons
3.   Work planned for next week
4.   Problems and opportunities present or anticipated

The project manager submits a Project Status Summary, usually bi-weekly, (see the example below).

* The symbols +, X and # are inserted in the cells under *Before* and *Now* for information items 1, 2. 3. and 4.

Project Status Summary						
Project:			**Project Mgr:**			**Date:**
Start Date		**Original End Date**			**New End Date**	
					User	
Before*	**Essential Element of Information**	**Now***	**Yes**	**No**	**Notified**	**Approved**
	1. Meeting Performance. Rqmts		/////			
	2. On Schedule					
	3. Within Present Budget					
	A. Overrun coming?					
	B. Scope change?					
	a. Change authorized?					
	b. Resources required?					
	c. Work started?					
	4. Adequate budget?					

Explanation and action required for +, X and #
    + = performance proceeding per objectives
    X = qualified answer, needs attentions, problem likely
    # = "out of control" situations influencing the meeting of project objectives						

Significant Accomplishments						
Upcoming Milestones		**Time Periods (week/month)**				

When a Project is in Trouble

- Schedules have slipped (overruns or distractions)
    - o People are being added or considered
    - o Task work is being scheduled after hours and on weekends
- Confidence in project plans is waning
- Remaining work is not well defined
- User participation is deteriorating – especially relative to quality reviews
- Important tasks are overlooked
- Re-work is mounting
- Documentation is being postponed
- Staff is confused and assignments are re-worked.

Getting Out of Trouble

- Find where you are – **really**
    - o Get lists of tasks and deliverables
    - o Set up *repository* and insert existing deliverables
    - o Define *gaps* to be filled
- Estimate costs and lead times to fill gaps
- Estimate and schedule the remainder of the project
    - o Insist on a full time staff
    - o Assume the project will be done right the first time.
- If the schedule is unacceptable,
    - o Try to reduce the scope of the system
    - o Add people only if task dependencies make it practical
    - o Make judicious quality compromises only as a last resort

How to Recognize Success

- Executives/users *sell* project results and feel good about setting all priorities
- Executives/users monitor costs and quality
- Users are pleased with project results and say so
- Projects are rarely late or over budget
- Documentation is always complete and up-to-date
- Changes are controlled with minimum rework
- You always know where things stand

Project Administration

Setting up Project Administration

It is suggested that a *Project Administration Document (PAD)* be set up, perhaps by the *Project Administrator*. This can be in the form of a loose-leaf binder that holds all of the administrative paperwork relevant to the project. It is a good idea that pre-formatted contents be used (many of which are included in this book). That way the administrative records will be found in the same section for any project. Setting up the PAD is simply a matter of preparing the required index tabs in accordance with the format adopted by the organization.

Here is the kind of information kept in the Project Administration Document:
- Project requests and approvals
- Project schedules, costs and plans
- Action notifications
- Development change requests
- Project status
- Project reviews
- And more

6. Controlling the Project

Most marketing projects are complex undertakings, requiring strong management skills and disciplines. In particular, the project must be closely monitored. The project control function must assure that:
- All important tasks continue to be defined and assigned.
- Task completion dates are consistent with the resources available as the project unfolds.
- Progress is measured.
- Additional resources are made available when needed and justified.
- The project is completed on time and within budget.

At the end of Chapter 7 we present a project control tool for providing this level of control for a project. It is in the form of a set of checklists by which management can measure the work that is being done on the project and get a clear picture of what work remains and when it can be expected to be completed.

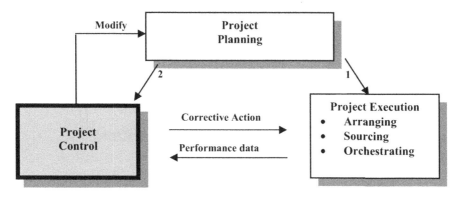

1 indicates that project planning specifies the project activities.
2 indicates that project planning specifies the control activities and the control criteria.

The project control element receives performance data from the project execution element. If something is amiss, and project control determines that it is the result of an execution problem, corrective action is specified to the project execution element.

If project control determines that it is the result of an imperfect plan, directives to modify the plan are sent to the project planning element.

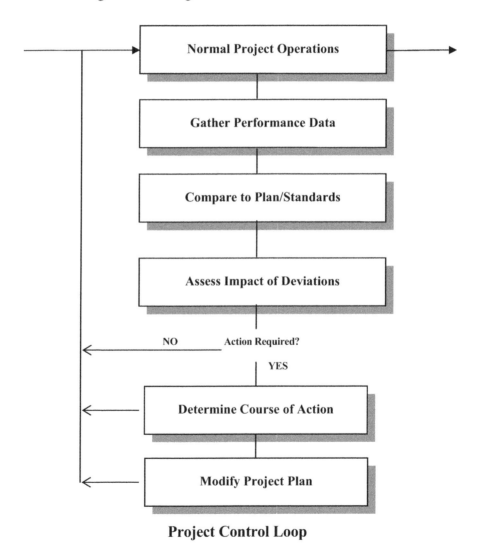

Michael W. Lodato Ph. D.

Elements to be controlled The four principal elements to be monitored closely are:

- Product quality
- Schedule attainment
- Budget attainment
- Use of resources

Project Control Loop The figure below shows a process recommended for monitoring and controlling these elements.

Normal Project Operations

Gather Performance Data

Compare to Plan/Standards

Assess Impact of Deviations

NO   Action Required?

YES

Determine Course of Action

Modify Project Plan

Project Control Loop

80

The third box down implies that performance has to be compared to something, such as the project plan and standards.

The fourth box and decision entry implies that not all deviations from plan and standards warrant a change. When action is required, the course of that action needs to be determined. Sometimes it is a change in the performance, such as a rework of some task or deliverable.

The last box indicates that sometimes the project plan itself has to be modified.

Ground Rules for Controlling
- First, prioritize the control variables. That is, determine what is most important to be controlled. Logically, product quality is a high priority issue.
- When the project is being done for a customer, marketing realities affect control, i.e. customer satisfaction takes importance.
- The control process should be exercised often.
- As deviations from plan or standards are encountered, the causes of the deviations should be examined so as to learn what can be done to prevent their reoccurrence.
- Solutions must be practical

Information Needed for Monitoring Here is a list of the things project managers work with in controlling a project.
- Evidence of task completion
- Actual completion dates
- Percentage of completion estimates on tasks yet uncompleted
- Product quality descriptions
- Actual resource usage, including time reports
- Environmental information, such as actual team size, actual team experience level, number of users involved in the project, actual time away from the project by project participants. Assumptions about these things should have been documented when the work effort estimates were done and should be available for comparison with the actual results.

Gathering of Project Information for Control There are two types of reporting used for control:
- Event-driven reporting. This is reporting on such events, as they occur, as task releases, major deliverables produced; end of phases, quality reviews, change of project scope, and changes to project plans.

- <u>Calendar-driven reporting.</u> Examples of this kind of reporting are:
  - o Project staff reports their time and progress on each assigned task, perhaps weekly. This includes the estimated time-to-completion on each task.
  - o Project manager reports on budget, schedule and status, perhaps bi-weekly. This includes monitoring of the impact of performance on the schedule and budget.

Formal Monitoring There is a formal project control process that is recommended.

- The project plan should contain logical *checkpoints*, for example
  - o Predetermined dates, such as at the end of a month or during an executive's regular meeting, or regular quality review meetings.
  - o Anticipated events, such as the end of phases, completion of testing of a major deliverable.
- At each *checkpoint* there is a meeting at which progress and achievements are reported. It is important that participants at such meetings should be well prepared.
- Standard checkpoint questions can be helpful. Examples:
  - o What specific work tasks have been completed?
  - o Was the work effort greater or less than expected?
  - o Can the work plan be balanced to future performance?
  - o Are there any special requirements that need support?
  - o What should be the performance goals for next status meeting?
  - o Do you foresee problems? Where?
  - o Are there any persistent problems? What are you doing about them?
  - o Are you getting everything you need?
  - o Are there any opportunities we can exploit?
  - o Are the people assigned to the project actually working on the project?
  - o Is the budget sufficient?
  - o Is the schedule realistic?
  - o Have you made changes that are not reflected in the project plan?
  - o Do you have any other comments?

The Project Manager's Tools for Control   The project plan is an invaluable tool for the project manager in performing his/her project control function. It contains:

- The work breakdown
- The flow plan
- The estimate
- The schedule

Of course documentation, programming, testing and other standards are also important.

Project Quality Assurance

Quality Review Flow

Control should be exercised at three levels: task, phase and system, product launch or other major project result. The following graphic shows the flow of interactions as the quality review (QR) process is exercised. For the sake of completeness, it includes the project execution flow covered earlier.

For task level control we start with Step 3 on the graphic, where, in Step 4, the project manager reviews the results of the work effort, as found in the project repository. He/she first reviews for errors or omissions and prepares responses to open points. The project manager then judges
>   (a.) how the work is progressing on the tasks,
>   (b) if all pertinent data has been gathered,
>   (c) if the task is completed and
>   (d) if we can go to the next task.
If he/she finds the task results acceptable, they are placed in the Project Repository.

Some results call for more in-depth review. In this case the project manager may call on evaluators to help in assessing quality (Step 5). If they deem that the results are inadequate or inaccurate, they re-release the task to the project team for rework.

If the evaluators deem the work is OK, they forward the results on to the Quality Review Committee with appropriate comments, suggestions and recommendations. This may be done via a briefing given to the QR team. The Quality Review Committee (Step 6) either accepts the quality and authorizes the release of the next batch of tasks or instructs the project team, through the project manager, to rework the tasks in question.

Periodically, status and time reports are submitted to the project manager who, on a regular basis, submits status, cost and schedule reports.

Phase level control is exercised after the results of tasks have been reviewed and approved and after the phase-end document has been prepared. Here there is a final review of the final phase results to determine if the contents are of sufficient quality to proceed to the next phase.

One final level of control is needed and that is the level that turns the system over to the users, product over to the marketplace or produces other major project results and ends the project. This results in a formal turnover to the users and achieving certification that the system is accepted by them.

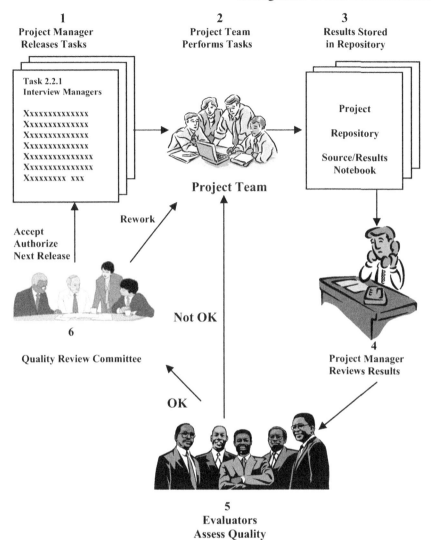

1
Project Manager
Releases Tasks

2
Project Team
Performs Tasks

3
Results Stored
in Repository

Task 2.2.1
Interview Managers

Xxxxxxxxxxxxxx
Xxxxxxxxxxxxxx
Xxxxxxxxxxxxxx
Xxxxxxxxxxxxxx
Xxxxxxxxxxxxxx
Xxxxxxxxxxxxxx
Xxxxxxxxx xxx

Project

Repository

Source/Results
Notebook

Project Team

Rework

Accept
Authorize
Next Release

6

Quality Review Committee

Not OK

4
Project Manager
Reviews Results

OK

5
Evaluators
Assess Quality

There are some steps that should be carried out by those conducting the evaluations. They are:

- Check that all documentation is complete
- Get a *feel* for the system, product launch or other major project result and its goals
- Examine each deliverable and comment on it
- Apply the documentation standards to the deliverables
- Prepare a brief evaluation report
- Review the findings with the project manager and give him/her a chance to make corrections

- Then revise the evaluation and distribute the findings
- Present the evaluation to the Quality Review Committee.

Conducting the Quality Review Meetings

- Prepare an agenda
- Send an announcement
- Prepare a presentation checklist
- Have the project manager serve as the discussion leader, covering:
  - o Project overview
  - o Meeting objectives
  - o Walkthrough of the launch or system
  - o Proof of completion of action items
  - o Evaluator's report on the documentation review
  - o Acceptance of the findings or action items
- Prepare the meeting minutes and distribute them
- Conduct a follow-up meeting if one is necessary

Prerequisites for Good Quality Assurance

- A commitment to quality by both user management and technical management.
- Good project documentation with standards to guide in its creation and assessment
- User participation
- Right psychological atmosphere

General Approach to Quality Assurance

- The QA team should be objective in its review and therefore should not be a part of the project. Team members should be selected for their common sense, foresight, flexibility, tact and sense of professionalism
- Either the project manager or the steering committee should initiate QA checkpoints.

Why Have Quality Reviews

- User involvement implies solving the business problem
- Yields higher quality project results
- Enforces documentation creation and quality
- Limits jumping ahead and the resulting rework

Who is Involved in Quality Reviews

- The project sponsor who:
  - o Serves as chairman of the QA Committee

- o   Is responsible that the launch will be successful or the system solves the business problem
  - o   Approves the work done
  - o   Has the authority to stop the project
- The Project Manager who:
  - o   Readies all results for review
  - o   Provides results to evaluators
  - o   Sets up and runs the QA meetings
- The evaluators who assess quality and adherence to standards
- The Quality Assurance Committee, which accepts or rejects the results using inputs from evaluators.

Policies Supporting Quality Reviews

- Quality reviews are built into the project life cycle
- Quality will not be sacrificed. Standards will be followed. If the users lose interest, the project manager should "park" the project.
- The project sponsor has the authority to:
  - o   Approve the proposal and project plans
  - o   Approve quality reviews
  - o   Halt the project
  - o   Accept the system, product launch or other major project result

7. Product Launch Management

Why Product Launches Are So Difficult To Pull Off

When was the last time, if ever, that you observed a really successful launch of a product? Almost every company, including the big ones, botches the launch.

The Better Mouse Trap is a Myth. *Build a better mousetrap, and the world will beat a path to your door* is a myth -- always has been. But the small amount of detailed attention that a lot of companies give to a product launch seems to indicate that they think that having a great technical product is enough. We know that the best technology alone does not guarantee business success. Superior technology may be necessary for success but it is not sufficient. You must also have first-rate marketing, sales, distribution and support.

There are reasons why newly launched products fail to meet expectations

Here is a list of some of them.
- Missing a market window. E.g. Pontiac's *Fiero* that was ahead of its time. It missed its window on the front end. You can also be too late to market.
- Poor positioning. E.g. Cocoa Cola's *Classic Coke.* Consumer expectations were not developed.
- Product failure. E.g. An earlier model of the Audi that had many functional problems.
- Shifts in purchasing habits. We've seen the *baby boomers* make several shifts.
- Market changes. The market for cigarettes has changed dramatically in recent years.
- Under-investment. Not staying with the product long enough.
- Invisibility. Not investing enough in promotion.
- Economic dislocations. E.g. Recessions.
- Poor channel support.
- Misread competition. E.g. US semiconductor industry misread competition from Japan.

- No industry support. Lacking validation by industry gurus and analysts.
- Misunderstanding of real customer needs.
- Political upheavals. E.g. Terrorist attacks and wars.

Not all of these can be anticipated but if the launch is well managed the company can respond to them better.

The Magnitude of the Product Launch Challenge

A product launch is a tremendous project management challenge deserving of high quality management effort. All the components of your offering: product, service, pricing, support, distribution, etc. have to be in place and coordinated ·at launch time. They must be introduced with first rate positioning, promotion, marketing and sales. Execution of each function must' be crisp -- on time and on target. As illustrated by the following two graphics, a lot of major things have to come together at launch time.

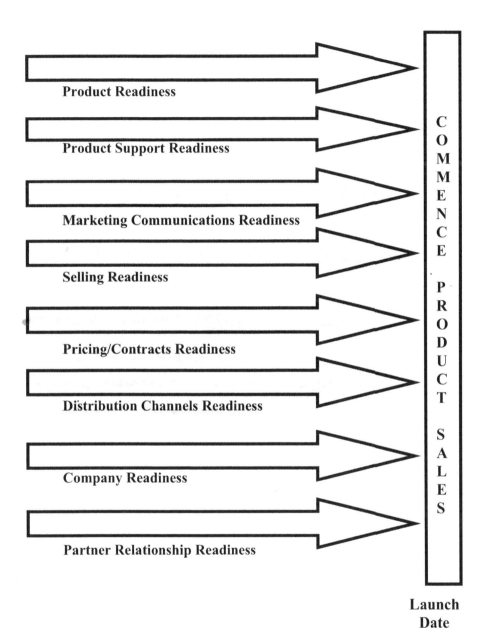

Figure 7-A

Using functional flow block diagramming, the top level would look like this.

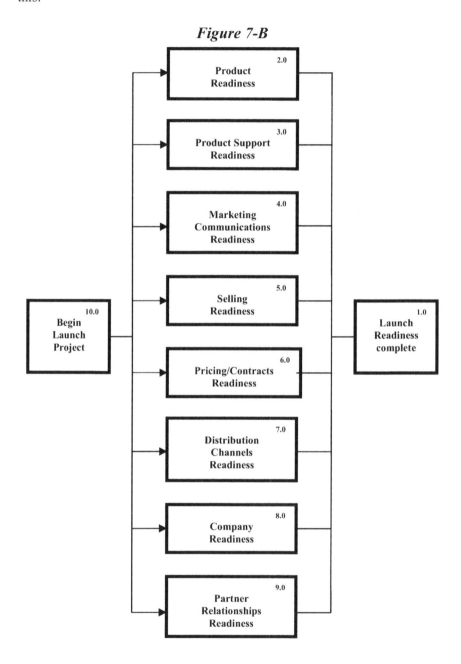

Figure 7-B

Product Readiness deals with the effort that must be expended to assure that all components of the offering are ready, quality assured and tested at launch. This includes the products themselves, the packaging, user and technical support documentation and demonstration packages.

Product Support Readiness deals with the effort that must be expended so that training materials are available, training is conducted and support tools are provided for the people who will support customers of the products.

Marketing Communications Readiness deals with a wide variety of promotional activities and results that have to occur and be coordinated prior to the launch date. These include broad-based promotion such as print ads, articles and white papers, brochures, web site use, publicity releases and trade shows, and focused promotion efforts such as telemarketing, direct mail and seminars. For maximum effect, the different activities should be synchronized. For example, media ads should be synchronized with PR and direct response activities.

Marketing communications should have a market focus so that all efforts and activities are directed at the target markets for the products.

Selling Readiness deals with having enough fully-trained salespeople to meet sales goals, having a formal sales management process to guide their efforts, sales tool development, sales skills training, training on giving demonstrations, proposal guides and a sales support organization ready to handle lead management. Assessment of the competition for the products may also be included.

Pricing/Contracts Readiness deals with having well documented pricing objectives, policies, methods and price schedules along with contract terms and conditions so that sales can be made at launch time. Financing options for purchasing the products may be included.

Distribution Channels Readiness deals with having enough marketing intermediaries, such as distributors and resellers, to reach the goals for selling through the channel. It includes recruiting and training of the channel members and having a group ready to support them on an on-going basis.

Company Readiness deals with activities that assure there is a company-wide understanding of how customers benefit from the new products and how employees can play a role in the success of the launch.

Partner Relationships Readiness deals with relationships, other than the channel type, that are part of the product marketing strategy. Such relationships are often referred to as strategic alliances. An example is the strategic alliances that IBM had with Intel and Microsoft when it launched the personal computer in 1981. Strategic alliances will not be covered in this chapter at this time.

Fail to Plan, Plan to Fail.

In my opinion, the main reason why product launches fail is the unwillingness, or inability, of management to prepare detailed product launch plans, monitor performance against those plans, and take corrective action when it is called for. In other words the management of the launch effort is ineffective.

No project can be successfully managed until the work content has been defined, broken down into chewable bite-sized tasks, estimated and staffed. Task durations need to be calculated and task dependencies (i.e. precedence relationships) must be made explicit so that a realistic schedule can be projected.

There are many, many deliverables, besides the product itself, that must be produced by the launch project. For example, there are press releases, ads, product sheets, telemarketing scripts, and much, much more. It's obvious that most of the deliverables are interrelated, making their creation even more challenging.

The attitude seems to be: when the product is ready, so will everything else. When I've conducted audits of launch readiness, not only were key tasks not completed, they weren't even defined and/or assigned.

At a minimum, you should have a checklist of all the deliverables and activities for the launch. The checklist the author has used contains over 100 items

All that sounds very complicated, doesn't it? Well, that's because it is.

I've seen product launches conducted in the absence of a product launch plan but with no documented product plan either. And so, there were no clear documented answers to questions like:
- *Who are the prospects and where are they?*
- *Why should they buy the product?*
- *How much will they pay*

- *What kind of sales force is needed?*
- *How will we support customers (and/or dealers)?*
- *Do we have adequate sales materials?*
- *How will the product (and company) be positioned?*
- *How will leads be generated and handled?*
- *How does the product compare with the competition?*
- *What is our company/product story?*

The Remedy -- A Product Launch Management Methodology

What every company that launches products needs is a product launch management methodology that guides the whole launch management effort in a way that leaves nothing to chance. It should be comprehensive enough to identify everything that should be done for a launch to be successful, the order in which they should be done, the effort and lead times involved, and the interrelationships among tasks (coordination). The methodology should guide in addressing strategic issues -- such as target markets, pricing, and positioning -- and tactical ones -- such as PR and advertising, training of the sales people, lead handling, sales and product literature and the like. All of this has to be planned and managed so that things come together at the right times.

Developing a methodology is tough work, but it is worth doing. A well-executed launch makes the difference between a product that survives and prospers and one that falls short of expectations. This chapter provides an example of a product launch management methodology.

Benefits With a launch management methodology you can expect to develop comprehensive launch plans with less effort and in less time. With sound launch plans you will be able to:
- Coordinate all launch activities better and track progress
- Execute launches at much lower cost and higher efficiency
- Set realistic launch dates
- Eliminate costly surprises
- Get the product to market sooner
- Generate more qualified leads sooner
- Handle the prospect volume and convert it into sales
- Support the product once it is shipped; and finally
- Increase company profitability.

Overview of Product Launch Management

Launch management is a form of project management. It therefore consists of three major functions:
1. Launch *planning*,
2. Staffing for and *executing* the plans, and
3. *Controlling* the effort by measuring performance and making adjustments

The accompanying figure shows these three elements of product launch management. Arrow 1 indicates that *Launch Planning* specifies the launch activities.   Arrow 2 indicates that *Launch Planning* also specifies the launch control activities and criteria.

When things aren't proceeding as expected, sometimes the execution activities must be adjusted; other times the launch plan needs to be modified.

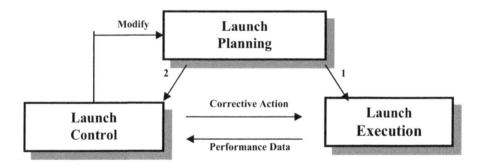

The goal of this management process is to assure that everything is carried out that will make the newly launched product a success – the plans, organization, management processes, people, offerings, promotional material, advertising, publicity, sales support, etc.

Product Launch Planning

The product launch plan consists of:
- Specifying the requirements for a successful launch
- Setting up the launch project organization.
- Defining the tasks required to satisfy those requirements

- Assigning tasks to individuals.
- Estimating the man-hours and durations associated with each task
- Specifying task dependencies, i.e. the order in which tasks should be done
- Laying out the project schedule

The Product Launch Manager tailors the product launch project plan from the launch tasks, procedures and controls contained in these guidelines and then uses the task descriptions in working on and directing the project activities.

In assigning tasks, one of those assigned should be listed as *Task Leader.*

Based on their availability - half time, full-time, or other - estimate the duration of each task.

Determine the precedence relationships among the tasks – tasks that must follow completion of other tasks and tasks that can be done concurrently – and use this information to estimate milestone dates such as the completion of phases.

Assemble all of the tasks into a coordinated plan, get management approval and publish the plan.

Requirements for a Launch to be Successful (Readiness Checklists)

In this section is a menu of requirements that could be a part of a particular product launch. These are capabilities that should be in place at the time of the launch of the product. The planner should check those that apply and add others that are relevant. There is no claim by the author that the list is comprehensive.

The requirements are organized into categories, including 7 of the 8 categories shown on *Figure 7-A*, for ease of understanding and to make it easier to identify requirements that are not on the list. The list is influenced by the fact that most of the author's experience has been with software products.

Because of time and resource constraints, it may not be possible to satisfy all of the readiness requirements or to do all the tasks leading to their satisfaction. Failure to do so, of course, reduces the chances for a successful launch. But taking risks is not rare for executives. What **is** important is that the risks are understood before they are undertaken. The product launch methodology, particularly the project control tool introduced later, is meant to give visibility of potential risks.

Product Readiness Requirements:

- Fully tested, quality assured, attractively packaged products, ready for delivery
- High quality end user and technical support documentation.
- Production procedures for making the products
- Demonstration packages consisting of software, sample data and instructions
- Procedures for shipping and configuration control

Product Support Readiness Requirements:

- A product training program for internal training
- Customer training materials for training users, trainers and technical support personnel of customers
- Product technical support manuals
- Adequate number of product/technical support staff
- A capability to support field sales with telephone support

Marketing Communications Readiness Requirements

- A well thought out statement positioning the product (line) in the market place.
- A marketplace and the media conditioned by public relations to expect the product (line)
- An advertising program ready to be implemented, with space in key media reserved for insertion, an ad placement schedule synchronized with PR and direct mail and a budget to support the program.
- Direct mail pieces to support a combined direct mail/telemarketing campaign.
- Brochures, product data sheets, scripted presentation materials, sample cover letters, success stories and other sales tools.
- Feature articles for publication
- Procedures for controlled dissemination of information regarding company products and programs. (Needed to maintain credibility and minimize the impact of competitors' actions)
- A trade show program
- A public seminar program

Selling Readiness Requirements:

- A documented structured selling process that is understood and followed by sales and sales support personnel and their managers.
- Fully trained sales people in sufficient numbers to meet sales goals.
- A fully staffed and trained sales support organization, ready to handle inquiries, qualify leads, hand them off to field sales and track and report sales activity.
- Fully trained field technical sales support people.
- Fully trained field applications sales support people.
- Fully trained home-based technical sales support people.
- Fully trained home-based applications sales support people.
- Enough fully trained sales administrators prepared to handle sales orders.
- Enough fully trained customer support people.
- Enough fully trained telemarketers with scripts and tools to handle incoming inquiries as well as outgoing prospect qualification calls.
- Brochures, product data sheets, scripted presentation materials, sample cover letters, success stories and other sales tools.
- Descriptions of target accounts and profiles of target prospects.
- Territory assignments and compensation plans, including sales and support incentive programs.
- Sales forecasts (goals).
- Comparisons with competitive offerings (price, features, technology) and competition knock-offs.

Pricing/Contracts Readiness Requirements:

- A pricing strategy for the product (line)
- Contract terms and conditions, including warranty
- Price schedules with terms and conditions of the sale.

Distribution Channels Readiness Requirements:

- A distribution channel plan for the product (line)
- Adequate number of trained channel partners
- An effective channel support program

Michael W. Lodato Ph. D.

Company Readiness Requirements
- A company-wide understanding of how customers benefit from the new products and how employees can play an important role in its success of the launch.

Setting up the Launch Project Organization

O verall management of the launch will be the responsibility of the head of Product Marketing, with a major delegation of this responsibility to the Product Manager for the product (line) being launched. This person often serves as the Product Launch Manager (PLM).

Product Launch Manager (PLM)

The Product Launch Manager is the person who has the overall responsibility for the product launch project. The Product Launch Manager shall have responsibility for:
- Launch planning and management.
- Procedures for controlled dissemination of information and announcements.

Product Launch Committee (PLC)

The PLM works closely with the PLC throughout the project. The PLC normally consists of some sales executives, product marketing representatives, and others. Not all PLC members are involved in each launch activity, but they should be present at the kickoff to understand the scope of the product launch project and agree on the scope and timetable.

Product Launch Administrator (PLA)

As with any project of significance there are a lot of administrative things to be handled, including the scheduling of meetings, issuing of memoranda, and maintaining the product launch repository. These are taken care of by the PLA.

Building the Needed Capabilities

T his section lists the tasks that should be undertaken to build the needed capabilities for a successful launch of the product.

Background

The underlying premise of a product launch is that the product includes not only the deliverable, tangible product and related documentation but also all of the company's associated services aimed at providing customers with maximum satisfaction.

The majority of product successes, and conversely, of failures are based upon the quality of work done regarding definition of the prospective users and their specific needs. Therefore some product launches are segmented into two phases.

Phase 1, Launch Test, will try out the product concepts, sales policies, promotion and the company's infrastructure on a pilot basis to assure that they are on target. The objective is to validate the fit between product and market. This will assure a higher probability of success before betting more resources on a full-scale launch.

We are suggesting, for example, that Phase 1 employ focus groups to get as accurate a picture as possible regarding market acceptance of the concept and price sensitivity.

Phase 2, Execution, focuses on rolling out the production product and application of all planned Company resources to meet performance goals. It is during Phase 2 that all the capabilities listed above under requirements are put in place.

Departmental Roles

A successful launch will require understanding of the roles to be played by and coordination among each organizational unit: Product Development, Sales, Product Marketing, Technical Marketing, Customer Support, and Administration. Each must establish objectives, allocate staff time and set budgets relative to the needed capabilities listed above under requirements for a launch to be successful.

As an initial allocation of responsibilities for the needed capabilities:

The head of product marketing shall have responsibility for:
- Development of the organizational structure and the duties and accountabilities of each of his/her direct reports.

Sales shall take responsibility for:

101

- Development and approval of the sales plan as it relates to the product (line) being launched.
- Implementation of the sales and sales management processes.
- Sales staffing and training.
- Sales support staffing and training.
- Preparation of sales administration to handle orders
- Preparation of the telemarketing group with scripts and other aids .
- Territory assignments and compensation plans.
- Sales forecasts.

Product Marketing shall take responsibility for:
- A company-wide understanding of the product offering, why prospects and customers will buy the product, and how employees play an important role in its success.
- Development of positioning statements and translation of same into messages to be transmitted to the marketplace, industry and the company
- Maintenance and dissemination of competitive information and competitive comparisons..
- Descriptions of target accounts and profiles of target prospects.
- Public relations
- Feature articles for publication.
- Price schedules and terms and conditions of the sale - (in conjunction with other departments).
- The advertising program - (In conjunction with Marketing Communications).
- Direct mail pieces and their use (In conjunction with PR and advertising.)
- Brochures, scripted presentation materials, sample cover letters, success stories and other sales tools.
- The trade show program.
- The public seminar program.

Technical Marketing shall have responsibility for:
- Product data sheets.
- Staffing and training of the technical marketing and field systems engineering groups.
- Readiness of the products and documentation.
- Demonstration packages consisting of software, sample data and instructions.
- Interface with Product Marketing Management.
- Proposal procedures.

Customer Support shall have responsibility for
- Customer support staffing and training
- Customer training materials
- Production procedures to make, ship and control configurations.

Launch Program Tasks

Below is a fairly exhaustive list of tasks that might be undertaken during a product launch project. Very few companies would have the budget or time to do all of these tasks. They are presented so that the readers can select a subset they can afford to do - the tasks that are the most important and relevant.

The task lists have columns for *Task Number, Task Name,* and *Due Date.* Some tasks continue throughout the launch project. This is noted by writing the word *duration* in the due date column.

The *Assigned* column is used to write the name of the task leader when it is known. The *Complete* column has checkboxes to indicate that a task has been completed.

LAUNCH PROGRAM TASKS

TASK NO.	TASK NAME	ASSIGNED	DUE DATE	COMPLETE
Launch Management Tasks (LM)				
LM1.0	Develop Launch Plan			[ ]
LM2.0	Conduct Launch Kickoff Meeting			[ ]
LM3.0	Manage the Launch		Duration	[ ]
LM4.0	Evaluate Progress/Success of the Launch		Duration	[ ]
Organizational Tasks (OR)				
OR1.0	Appoint Product Launch Manager (PLM)			[ ]
OR1.1	Organize Product Launch committee (PLC)			[ ]
OR2.0	Make Departmental Transfers (Where Appropriate)			[ ]
OR2.1	Hire/Reduce Staff Where Needed			[ ]
OR3.0	Set up Coordination with Sales Administration			[ ]
OR4.0	Distribute Organization Plan w. Responsibilities			[ ]

LAUNCH PROGRAM TASKS

TASK NO.	TASK NAME	ASSIGNED	DUE DATE	COMPLETE

Planning Related Tasks (PL)

PL1.0	Conduct Market/Industry Research			[ ]
PL1.1	Conduct Focus Groups			[ ]
PL1.2	Interview Customers			[ ]
PL2.0	Determine Target Markets for Product (Line)			[ ]
PL3.0	Conduct Competitive Evaluation			[ ]
PL4.0	Document Product Marketing Plan			[ ]
PL4.1	Document Technical Marketing Plan			[ ]
PL5.0	Prepare Initial Sales Forecasts &/or Budgets			[ ]
PL6.0	Draft Initial Financial Pro Forma Statements			[ ]
PL6.1	Approve Financial Projections and Budgets			[ ]
PL7.0	Develop Customer Launch Plan			[ ]
PL7.1	Develop Strategies for Each Major Account			[ ]

Product Related Tasks (PR)

PR1.0	Name the Product (line) (do legal name search)			[ ]
PR1.1	Finalize Product Model Designations			[ ]
PR1.2	Develop Product Packaging and Delivery Packages			[ ]
PR1.3	Develop Graphics & Overall Look of Packaging			[ ]
PR2.0	Develop Procedures for Shipping & Configuration Control			[ ]
PR3.0	Finalize Testing and Quality Assurance			[ ]
PR3.1	Set QA Test Parameters			[ ]
PL3.2	Conduct Alpha Tests			[ ]
PL3.3	Conduct Beta Tests			[ ]
PL3.4	Implement Change Control			[ ]
PR3.5	Test Documentation			[ ]
PR3.6	Produce Product Documentation (technical & end user)			[ ]
PR4.0	Produce Products			[ ]
PR5.0	Produce Product Demonstration Packages			[ ]
PR6.0	Develop Product Training Program			[ ]
PR6.1	Conduct Product Training			[ ]

Product Support Related Tasks (PS)

PS1.0	Develop Product Technical Support Manuals			[ ]
PS1.1	Develop Customer Support Training Materials			[ ]
PS2.0	Develop/Conduct Customer Support Skills Training Program			[ ]
PS3.0	Augment Product/Technical Support Staff			[ ]
PS4.0	Coordinate Development of Product Data Sheets			[ ]
PS5.0	Establish Telephone Support to Field Sales			[ ]

LAUNCH PROGRAM TASKS

TASK NO.	TASK NAME	ASSIGNED	DUE DATE	COMPLETE

Marketing Communications Related Tasks (MC)

MC1.0	Develop Messages Aimed At the Market			[ ]
MC1.1	Achieve Consensus on Positioning Messages			[ ]
MC2.0	Establish Public Relations Plan			[ ]
MC2.1	Coordinate Preparation of Press Releases			[ ]
MC2.2	Develop Product Backgrounder			[ ]
MC2.3	Plan and Conduct Trade Journal & Analyst Briefings			[ ]
MC2.4	Follow Up To Media and Analysts			[ ]
MC2.5	Organize "Speakers Bureau"/Pick spokespersons			[ ]
MC3.0	Coordinate Ad/PR w. Market'g Communications Dept		Duration	[ ]
MC3.1	Select Media for ads			[ ]
MC3.2	Coordinate Advertising Plan, including ad placement schedule			[ ]
MC3.3	Design Advertising Pieces			[ ]
MC3.4	Coordinate Media Insertion Schedule (Synchronized with PR)			[ ]
MC4.0	Develop Direct Mail List			[ ]
MC4.1	Design Direct Mail Pieces & Campaign. Including messages			[ ]
MC4.2	Conduct Direct Mail Releases			[ ]
MC5.0	Plan for Trade Show Participation (Sites, Dates, Logistics)			[ ]
MC6.0	Coordinate Design of Collateral Materials			[ ]
MC6.1	Coordinate Development of Brochures			[ ]
MC6.2	Produce Brochures, Data Sheets, Presentations & Other Tools			[ ]
MC6.3	Coordinate Timely Distribution of Materials			[ ]
MC7.0	Send Announcements to Customer Base			[ ]
MC7.1	Follow Up With Telephone Calls or Visits			[ ]
MC8.0	Plan Seminar Program (Sites, Dates, Logistics)			[ ]
MC8.1	Establish and Maintain the Product Repository		Duration	[ ]

Selling Readiness Related Tasks (SR)

SR1.0	Augment Sales Staff			[ ]
SR1.1	Develop Sales Skills Training Program			[ ]
SR1.2	Conduct Sales Skill Training			[ ]
SR2.0	Develop Sales Support Training Program			[ ]
SR2.1	Conduct Sales Support Training			[ ]
SR3.0	Develop Telemarketing Skills Training Program			[ ]
SR3.1	Develop Telemarketing Scripts			[ ]
SR3.2	Conduct Telemarketing Skills Training			[ ]
SR3.3	Develop Lead Management Process			[ ]
SR3.4	Conduct Lead Management Training (hand-off, tracking, reporting)			[ ]
SR4.0	Develop Sales Administration Training Program			[ ]

LAUNCH PROGRAM TASKS

TASK NO.	TASK NAME	ASSIGNED	DUE DATE	COMPLETE
SR4.1	Conduct Sales Administration Training			[ ]
SR5.0	Indoctrinate sales force on sales management process			[ ]
SR6.0	Distribute Sales Manuals/Forms to All Salespeople			[ ]
SR7.0	Indoctrinate All on Proposal Process			[ ]
SR7.1	Establish Point-of-Contacts for sales related questions			
	(Delivery, product performance, pricing, billing, promotions, etc.)			[ ]
SR8.0	Document Plan for Field Sales			[ ]
SR9.0	Document Comparisons with Competitive Products			[ ]
SR9.1	Document Competitive Knock Offs			[ ]
SR10.0	Prepare Sample Sales Letters			[ ]
SR11.0	Prepare Scripted Sales Presentation Materials			[ ]

Pricing/Contracts Related Tasks (C)

C1.0	Establish Pricing Strategy			[ ]
C1.1	Set Basis for Pricing (site, upgrade, purchase, lease)			[ ]
C1.2	Develop Pricing Schedule and Get Approval			[ ]
C1.3	Develop Contract Terms & Conditions; Get Approval			[ ]
C1.4	Develop a Product Warranty/Maintenance Offering			[ ]
C1.5	Print/Distribute Price Schedules and Contracts			[ ]

Distribution Channel Readiness Related Tasks (D)

D1.0	Develop Distribution Channel Plan			[ ]
D2.0	Recruit and Train Channel Participants			[ ]
D3.0	Develop Channel Support Program			[ ]

Company Readiness Related Tasks (CO)

CO1.0	Prepare Internal Launch Plan			[ ]
CO2.0	Make Arrangements for Internal Launch			[ ]
CO3.0	Release Internal Launch Announcement			[ ]
CO4.0	Conduct Kickoff Meeting for Sales/Marketing			[ ]
CO5.0	Conduct Internal Launch			[ ]

Some Comments about Marketing Communication Readiness

This section provides more information about the marketing communication readiness requirements. The following is the first level functional flow block diagram for this function. Refer to *Figure 7-B* for the top-level flow.

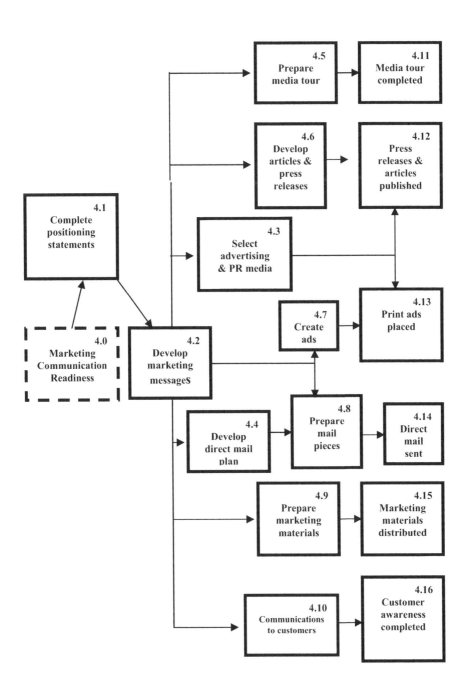

Some of these are at a task level, e.g. *4.5 Prepare Media Tour*, and therefore can be assigned. Others perhaps require the execution of several tasks and therefore can be represented by a second level functional flow. An example is *4.9 Prepare Marketing Materials*, which is drawn below.

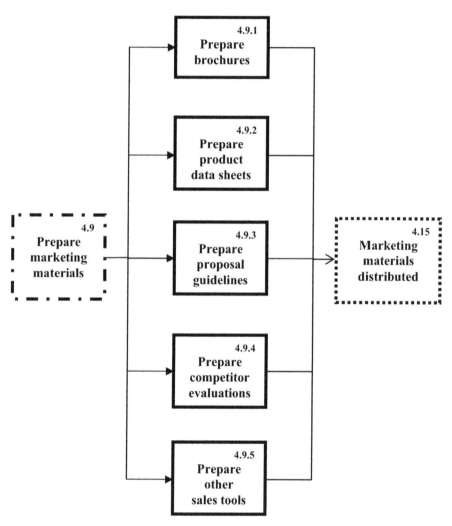

A good practice when drawing functional flows is define functions from the end (right) and back toward the reference box (left). Assign the box numbers after you have drawn and placed the boxes.

Similarly, you could draw a second level flow for the function *4.3 Select Ad & PR Media*. Here are some functions that might be included:

     4.3.1   Specify Ad and PR Objectives

4.3.2   Select Media and PR Outlets
4.3.3   Establish Budget for Advertising and PR
4.3.4   Create Advertising Plan
4.3.5   Create PR Plan
4.3.6   Review Editorial Calendars for PR
4.3.7   Make List of Alternative Advertising and PR Firms
4.3.8   Conduct Meetings with Candidate PR Firms
4.3.9   Determine Insertion Dates for PR Releases
4.3.10   Select PR Firm
4.3.11   Enter Contract With PR Firm
4.3.12   Conduct Meetings with Candidate Advertising Firms
4.3.13   Select Advertising Firm
4.3.14   Enter Contract with Advertising Firm

As you get down to the task level, follow the guidance given in *Chapter 4: The Project Planning Process* and document the task descriptions, estimate task durations and, using the networking procedures, prepare the launch project schedule.

Launch Information Repository: Some companies use a *Launch Information Repository*, which is a common source for all information to go into the various messages.   It is also used for control of the dissemination of information and announcements regarding company products and programs. (Note: this is critical to maintain credibility, minimize impact of competitor actions and get maximum positive exposure.) It contains:

- Features and benefits
- Competitive comparisons – price, features, technology
- Company background – principals, track record, financial status
- Positioning statements
- References
- Success stories
- Speakers bureau of designated company spokespersons
- Feature articles for publication

Marketing Communications Message Guide

The following table has been useful in assessing the scope of and organizing the task of development of marketing messages.

Michael W. Lodato Ph. D.

Marketing Communications Message Guide			
Audience	**Levels**	**Message Type***	**Desired Results**
The Company	Sales Development Support		Support for the program Market input from them
The Media	Editors Journalists Industry analysts Technical analysts		Company position Product position Proof concept is new & real
Current Customers	Executives Functional mgmt. Staff level		Buy the new product Buy other products Stay a customer
Prospects	Executives Functional mgmt. Staff level		Buy the new product Buy other products Displace competition
*Message types: POL - Policy paper – defines our position POS - Position paper – defines the product as a concept CON - Concept paper – defines implementation of the product CBK - Company backgrounder – used to support PR efforts PBK - Product backgrounder – used to support PR efforts UST - User stories PRI - Price, terms, availability			

Use the message type codes in the third column to indicate the type of message that is appropriate for the audience and the results desired.

Controlling the Product Launch Effort

As stated earlier, a product launch is a complex undertaking, requiring strong management skills and disciplines. In particular, the project must be closely monitored. This section provides the management control function for the project, assuring that:

- all important tasks continue to be defined and assigned.
- task completion dates are consistent with the resources available as the project unfolds,
- progress is measured,

- additional resources are made available when needed and justified,
- the project is completed on time and within budget.

Effective control is enhanced when progress is measured early and often. The following two figures illustrate the point.

The figure below depicts a situation where measurement of progress, say in terms of percentage of completion, was not made until about half way through the project and the actual percent of completion was only about half of what it should have been. In this case, one can make three assumptions about what can and should be done about this situation:

1. *Catch up Assumption:* We can catch up by the time the project reaches the original completion date. The figure indicates, by a fairly steep line, that to do this the pace of progress from this point will have to be increased significantly, not only from the actual pace but also from the originally planned pace..

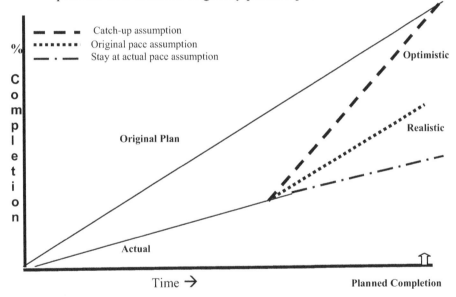

2. *Original Pace Assumption:* We can perform for the rest of the project at the original planned pace. So the original pace assumption line is shown as being parallel to the original plan line. You can see by the projection of this line that 100% completion will be far later than planned.

3. *Stay at Actual Pace Assumption:* We can't expect to make progress any faster that we have made to date. This is shown on the figure by an extension to the actual line. You can see that if

there was room, the figure would show that 100% completion would be very much later than planned.

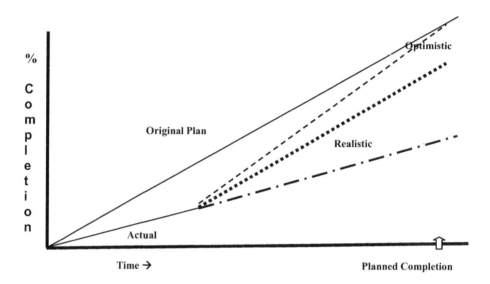

The second figure, above, depicts a situation where measurement of progress was made earlier, say about one-fourth of the way through the project, and the actual percent of completion was still only about half of what it should have been to that point. In this case:

1. *Catch up Assumption:* The catch up line is not as steep as in the first figure, but perhaps still overly optimistic.
2. *Original Pace Assumption:* This would still lead to the project being late, but not nearly as late as is the late measurement case.
3. *Stay at Actual Pace Assumption:* This would yield a project that was still significantly late.

Project Control Tool

Below is a methodology for providing this level of control for the project. It is a set of checklists for measuring the work that is being done on the project and for getting a clear picture of what work remains and when it can be expected to be completed.

You may choose not to use all of the readiness requirements shown because your project scope cannot accommodate all of them. Use what fits the situation. Here is how to use of the checklists.

The checklists consist of a set of *Readiness Requirements*, things that should be in place to succeed in meeting the goals for the product launch.

- If the requirement has been completely satisfied, simply check the box to the left of the requirement statement.
- If it has not been satisfied, refer to the related tasks that, once completed, would lead to satisfaction of the requirement.

There are 4 issues to be addressed relative to each related task identified:
1. Has the task been defined? If so, check the box.
2. Has it been assigned? If so, check the box and insert the assigned person's name.
3. Is there an agreed upon task completion date between the *Product Launch Manager (PLM)* and the task leader assigned, and does the task leader have enough resources and time to meet the date? If so, enter the due date.
4. Has the task been completed? If so, check the box.

When the *Completed* boxes for all the tasks are checked, the readiness requirement has been met and you can so indicate by putting a check in the readiness requirement box.

Space is provided for comments consisting of additional information that would clarify any of the entries made. For readiness requirements that have several tasks associated with them, it may be helpful to identify the tasks by letters (a., b., c.,..) and then use these identifiers when commenting on the tasks.

Deliverables from this effort should be incorporated into a three-ring binder, organized by the *Product Launch Administrator (PLA)*, so they are accessible to all that can benefit from them. The notebook can also serve as the repository for project deliverables.

Periodically, when the *PLM* and *PLA* meet with the *Product Launch Committee (PLC)*, they will use the *Checklists* to review whether tasks have been defined and assigned, and whether the due dates will be met, and in so doing get advanced warning of impending slippages and their impact on downstream tasks that need the deliverables from earlier tasks. With such visibility, management can assess whether additional resources or different methods might help make up some of the expected slippages, or at least update expectations in the company and in the marketplace.

At each project review, the completed checklist shows:
- what has been done,
- what remains to be done and
- when it is scheduled for completion.

It therefore is a form of a living plan.

PRODUCT LAUNCH READINESS CHECKLIST

READY   **READINESS REQUIREMENT**

[ ]   **An understanding of the needs of the marketplace and how the product (line) can fulfill those needs.**

RELATED TASKS	Assigned To:	Defin-ed	Assign-ed	Due Date	Complet-ed
Conduct primary research (E.g. focus groups, surveys, etc.)					
Purchase outside market research					
Assemble market information for ease of use					
Comments:					

READY   **READINESS REQUIREMENT**

[ ]   **Fully tested, quality assured product (line)**

RELATED TASKS	Assigned To:	Defin-ed	Assign-ed	Due Date	Complet-ed
Document test plan					
Conduct Alpha testing					
Conduct Beta testing					
Gather feedback on testing and take corrective action					
Conduct product review meeting to certify product for release					
Obtain management authorization for release					
Comments:					

PRODUCT LAUNCH READINESS CHECKLIST

READINESS REQUIREMENT

[ ] **Sufficient number of product units, attractively packaged with graphics, logo, etc., to satisfy the expected demand after launch.**

RELATED TASKS	Assigned To:	Defin-ed	Assign-ed	Due Date	Complet-ed
Document packaging requirements					
Design product packaging					
Design delivery packaging					
Forecast number of units needed for launch					
Arrange production of product units					
Produce the product packages					
Produce the delivery packages					
Comments:					

READINESS REQUIREMENT

[ ] **High quality end user and technical support documentation in sufficient quantities for the likely demand**

RELATED TASKS	Assigned To:	Defin-ed	Assign-ed	Due Date	Complet-ed
Document documentation requirements					
Design documentation style/look					
Draft end user documentation					
Draft technical support documentation					
Finalize end user documentation					
Finalize technical support documentation					
Forecast numbers needed for launch					
Arrange printing of both documents types					
Comments:					

PRODUCT LAUNCH READINESS CHECKLIST

READINESS REQUIREMENT

[ ]   **A fully documented sales and marketing plan for the product (line).**

RELATED TASKS	Assigned To:	Defin-ed	Assign-ed	Due Date	Complet-ed
Distribute sales & marketing plan annotated outline					
Specify sales and marketing goals					
Specify target markets & profiles					
Set unit sales projections					
Define territories and quotas					
Specify staffing plan					
Specify sales management plan					
Specify sales tactics					
Specify sales support plan					
Specify marketing communications plan					
Specify customer communications plan					
Conduct kickoff meeting for sales force					
Comments:					

116

PRODUCT LAUNCH READINESS CHECKLIST

READY   **READINESS REQUIREMENT**

[ ]   Clearly defined end user target markets for the product (line)

RELATED TASKS	Assigned To:	Defin-ed	Assign-ed	Due Date	Complet-ed
Develop market segmentation worksheet					
Conduct market segmentation					
Describe & analyze candidate segments					
Agree on target market criteria					
Document candidate profiles of target markets					
Identify specific companies that fit profiles					
Develop prospect qualification form					
Train salespeople on targeting and qualification					
Comments:					

READY   **READINESS REQUIREMENT**

[ ]   A well thought out set of arguments for positioning the product (line) within the end user and channel marketplace.

RELATED TASKS	Assigned To:	Defin-ed	Assign-ed	Due Date	Complet-ed
Draft end user positioning arguments					
Draft channel positioning arguments					
Draft concept paper					
Develop product level positioning					
Achieve consensus on positioning					
Produce concept paper`					
Train sellers on end user & channel positioning					
Develop and distribute positioning tools					
Comments:					

117

PRODUCT LAUNCH READINESS CHECKLIST

[ ]   A fully documented product marketing strategy for the product (line) in its markets

RELATED TASKS	Assigned To:	Defin-ed	Assign-ed	Due Date	Complet-ed
Prepare annotated outline for a product marketing strategy					
Prepare initial draft of product marketing strategy					
Get consensus on product. marketing strategy					
Issue final draft of product. marketing. strategy					
Comments:					

[ ]   A marketplace and the media conditioned by public relations to expect the product (line)

RELATED TASKS	Assigned To:	Defin-ed	Assign-ed	Due Date	Complet-ed
Develop list of media & market analysts					
Develop feature articles for publication					
Issue press releases					
Follow up with media & market analysts					
Comments:					

PRODUCT LAUNCH READINESS CHECKLIST

[ ]   A highly structured lead management process for the product (line)

RELATED TASKS	Assigned To:	Defin-ed	Assign-ed	Due Date	Complet-ed
Define lead management roles for telemarketing & telesales					
Develop prospect qualification form					
Identify key companies that fit profiles					
Define rules for assignment of leads					
Train salespeople on qualification					

Comments:

PRODUCT LAUNCH READINESS CHECKLIST

READY   **READINESS REQUIREMENT**

[ ]   Well documented and effective channel management process

RELATED TASKS	Assigned To:	Defin-ed	Assign-ed	Due Date	Complet-ed
Conduct market research to learn channel needs					
Draft channel recruiting cycle steps & support tools					
Draft simple reporting and forecasting					
Conduct brainstorming meeting on channel management.					
Distribute draft results of brainstorming sessions					
Achieve consensus on channel management process					
Document channel recruiting process					
Distribute channel management plan & procedures					
Train sales teams managing channels					
Comments:					

PRODUCT LAUNCH READINESS CHECKLIST

READY **READINESS REQUIREMENT**

[ ]   Clearly defined channel target markets for the product (line).

RELATED TASKS	Assigned To:	Defin-ed	Assign-ed	Due Date	Complet-ed
Develop market segmentation worksheet					
Conduct channel market segmentation					
Describe & analyze candidate segments					
Agree on channel target market criteria					
Document candidate profiles of target markets					
Identify specific companies that fit profiles					
Develop channel prospect qualification form					
Train salespeople on targeting and qualification					
Comments:					

PRODUCT LAUNCH READINESS CHECKLIST

READINESS REQUIREMENT

[ ] A fully documented channel sales and marketing plan

RELATED TASKS	Assigned To:	Defin-ed	Assign-ed	Due Date	Complet-ed
Specify channel sales and marketing goals					
Specify channel target markets & offerings					
Specify staffing plan					
Specify channel sales management plan					
Specify channel sales tactics					
Specify channel sales support plan					
Specify channel marketing communications plan					
Specify channel customer communications plan					
Conduct kickoff meeting for channel sales force					
Describe & analyze candidate channel segments					
Agree on channel target market criteria					
Document candidate profiles of channel target markets					
Identify specific channel companies that fit profiles					

Comments:

PRODUCT LAUNCH READINESS CHECKLIST

READY   **READINESS REQUIREMENT**

[ ] A sufficient number of channel partners ready to help achieve sales goals

RELATED TASKS	Assigned To:	Defin-ed	Assign-ed	Due Date	Complet-ed
Develop profile of desired channel partners					
Identify channel partner candidates					
Recruit channel partners					
Set up partner relationships with desired number of partners					
Conduct product training					
Conduct sales skills training					
Comments:					

READY   **READINESS REQUIREMENT**

[ ] Enough fully trained sales support people to handle inquiries, qualify leads and track and report on sales activity

RELATED TASKS	Assigned To:	Defin-ed	Assign-ed	Due Date	Complet-ed
Develop support training programs					
Determine number of support people needed					
Recruit additional support people, if needed					
Conduct product training					
Conduct sales support training					
Comments:					

123

PRODUCT LAUNCH READINESS CHECKLIST

READINESS REQUIREMENT

[ ] Enough fully trained technical support people, with support materials, to meet sales goals

RELATED TASKS	Assigned To:	Defin-ed	Assign-ed	Due Date	Complet-ed
Develop technical support training					
Develop technical support materials					
Determine number of technical support people needed					
Recruit additional technical. support people, if needed					
Distribute technical support materials					
Conduct product training					
Conduct technical support skills training					
Comments:					

PRODUCT LAUNCH READINESS CHECKLIST

READY   **READINESS REQUIREMENT**

[ ]   Enough fully trained customer support people, with support materials, to meet customer satisfaction goals

RELATED TASKS	Assigned To:	Defin-ed	Assign-ed	Due Date	Complet-ed
Develop customer support training					
Develop customer support materials					
Determine number of customer support people needed					
Recruit additional technical. support people, if needed					
Distribute customer support materials					
Conduct product training					
Conduct customer support skills training					
Comments:					

125

Michael W. Lodato Ph. D.

PRODUCT LAUNCH READINESS CHECKLIST

READINESS REQUIREMENT

[ ] Enough fully trained telemarketers, with scripts and tools, to handle incoming inquiries as well as outgoing prospect qualification calls

RELATED TASKS	Assigned To:	Defin-ed	Assign-ed	Due Date	Complet-ed
Develop telemarketing training					
Develop telemarketing scripts					
Determine number of telemarketing people needed					
Develop prospect qualification forms					
Recruit additional telemarketing people, if needed					
Distribute scripts and qualification forms					
Conduct product training					
Conduct telemarketing skills training					
Comments:					

READINESS REQUIREMENT

[ ] Enough fully trained sales administration people, to handle expected volume of proposals and orders

RELATED TASKS	Assigned To:	Defin-ed	Assign-ed	Due Date	Complet-ed
Develop sales administration training					
Determine number of sales administrators needed					
Recruit additional sales administrators, if needed					
Conduct sales administrator skills training					
Comments:					

126

PRODUCT LAUNCH READINESS CHECKLIST

READY **READINESS REQUIREMENT**

[ ] Enough fully trained salespeople to meet sales goals

RELATED TASKS	Assigned To:	Defin-ed	Assign-ed	Due Date	Complet-ed
Develop sales skills training programs					
Determine number of salespeople needed					
Develop product training program					
Recruit additional salespeople if needed					
Conduct product training					
Conduct sales skills training					
Comments:					

READY **READINESS REQUIREMENT**

[ ] A procedure and scripts for handling sales obstacles.

RELATED TASKS	Assigned To:	Defin-ed	Assign-ed	Due Date	Complet-ed
Document sales obstacles that are likely to be met					
Conduct training on obstacle handling					
Develop scripts for handling obstacles					
Comments:					

PRODUCT LAUNCH READINESS CHECKLIST

[ ]   Ready access by salespeople to all information they need to be successful.

RELATED TASKS	Assigned To:	Defin-ed	Assign-ed	Due Date	Complet-ed
Prepare annotated outline for a sales manual					
Make assignments for writing sections					
Edit submissions for inclusions					
Prepare and distribute sales manuals					
Comments:					

[ ]   Direct mail pieces to support a combined direct mail/telemarketing campaign of coordinated mailing and telephone follow up.

RELATED TASKS	Assigned To:	Defin-ed	Assign-ed	Due Date	Complet-ed
Decide direct mail messages					
Design direct mail pieces					
Purchase direct mail list					
Produce direct mail pieces					
Comments:					

PRODUCT LAUNCH READINESS CHECKLIST

READINESS REQUIREMENT

[ ]   **A promotional program ready to be implemented, with space in key media reserved for insertion, an ad placement schedule synchronized with PR and direct mail and a budget to support the program**

RELATED TASKS	Assigned To:	Defin-ed	Assign-ed	Due Date	Complet-ed
Set the promotional budget for the launch					
Recruit an advertising agency					
Recruit a public relations firm					
Develop messages aimed at target markets					
Determine the promotional mix consisting of advertising, PR, direct mail, Internet, etc.					
Select media for advertising					
Select media for PR releases					
Develop direct mail plan					
Prepare individual promotional pieces					
Prepare promotional implementation plan					
Implement promotional plan					
Develop measures of effectiveness of promotions					

Comments:

Michael W. Lodato Ph. D.

PRODUCT LAUNCH READINESS CHECKLIST

READINESS REQUIREMENT

[ ]   Understanding, by salespeople, of the competition for the products.

RELATED TASKS	Assigned To:	Defin-ed	Assign-ed	Due Date	Complet-ed
Document comparisons of the products with competitive products					
Document competitive knockoffs					
Conduct training of salespeople on the competition					
Comments:					

READY   **READINESS REQUIREMENT**

[ ]   Well thought out pricing, with price schedules and purchase agreement terms and conditions.

RELATED TASKS	Assigned To:	Defin-ed	Assign-ed	Due Date	Complet-ed
Determine pricing objectives					
Establish pricing policies					
Document pricing methodology and get approval					
Document and distribute pricing schedule					
Develop purchase agreement terms and conditions					
Print and distribute purchase agreements					
Comments:					

130

PRODUCT LAUNCH READINESS CHECKLIST

READY   **READINESS REQUIREMENT**

[ ]   **An ample supply of collateral material and other sales tools.**

RELATED TASKS	Assigned To:	Defin-ed	Assign-ed	Due Date	Complet-ed
Decide design of collateral material/tools					
Prepare the product brochures					
Prepare product data sheets					
Prepare sample sales letters					
Prepare scripted presentation materials					
Document success stories					
Develop video and audiotapes					
Arrange production of collateral material					
Produce and distribute enough copies of each to support anticipated marketing and sales activities					
Comments:					

PRODUCT LAUNCH READINESS CHECKLIST

READY **READINESS REQUIREMENT**

[ ] **Public seminar and trade shows program to support the sales development efforts.**

RELATED TASKS	Assigned To:	Defin-ed	Assign-ed	Due Date	Complet-ed
Develop public seminar and trade show program & budget related to sales efforts					
Develop seminar topics					
Develop strategy for use of seminars					
Make arrangements for seminars					
Develop measures of seminar success					
Decide which trade shows to participate in					
Make arrangements for trade shows participation					
Comments:					

Checklists as a Product Launch Audit Tool

It is advisable to conduct audits of the readiness for launch sometime after the execution of the launch project has begun. With an efficient launch readiness assessment process, similar to the one described above, several audits can be conducted for the same product launch. In particular, launch readiness audits should be conducted whenever a launch is underway in the absence of a comprehensive formal launch plan.

The author has used this checklist approach to help clients with launch efforts already underway. He created a checklist very similar to the one presented above. It showed what should be in place for the launch to be successful. He got the clients' agreement on this list. He then interviewed the launch manager, product manager and others involved in the launch to get the required information. He then submitted a report detailing, for each item on the checklist, his observations, evaluations and recommendations.

The results often showed that the product launch goals could not be met by the target launch date. But the visibility provided helped in salvaging a situation that would have become much worse.

It is **not** advisable for someone directly involved in the launch to serve as the auditor. Someone outside the project can be expected to be more objective.

At any time, before or during the interviewing, the auditor should feel free to add new readiness requirements and/or additional tasks

Here are just a few exhibits and comments from one of the product launch audit engagements. We will refer to the product being launched as Product N. Assume that the audit was conducted on 01/02/91.

[ ] **Enough fully trained salespeople to meet sales goals**

RELATED TASKS	Assigned To:	Defin-ed	Assign-ed	Due Date	Complet-ed
Develop sales skills training programs					
Determine number of salespeople needed	D. Wheeler				
Develop product training program	S. Benner	X	X	01/18/91	X
Recruit additional salespeople, if needed					X
Conduct product training	S. Benner	X	X	01/25/91	
Conduct sales skills training					

Comments:
D. Wheeler said that no additional salespeople are needed. A person will be identified for the sales skills training tasks within a week.
Note that the first and last tasks haven't even been defined. This is not an uncommon situation.

[ ] Enough fully trained customer support people, with support materials, to meet customer satisfaction goals

RELATED TASKS	Assigned To:	Defin-ed	Assign-ed	Due Date	Complet-ed
Develop customer support training	R. McKee	X	X	01/18/91	
Develop customer support materials	J. MacDonald	X	X	02/01/91	
Hire more customer support people	J. Boerman	X	X	01/25/91	
Distribute customer support materials	J. MacDonald	X	X	02/01/91	
Conduct customer support skills training	J. MacDonald	X	X	02/01/91	

Comments: As indicated, all tasks have been defined, assigned and given due dates. The need for additional customer support people will be determined as the launch project progresses. Then their hiring will be negotiated with the VP of Operations.

[ ] A fully documented product marketing strategy for Product N in its markets

RELATED TASKS	Assigned To:	Defin-ed	Assign-ed	Due Date	Complet-ed
Prepare annotated outline for a product marketing strategy					
Prepare initial draft of product marketing strategy					
Get consensus on product marketing strategy					
Issue final draft of product. marketing. strategy					

Comments: As indicated none of the above tasks have been defined, but at a recent meeting, D. Wheeler accepted the task of preparing an annotated outline and to make assignments for preparation of sections of the initial draft.

[ ]   An understanding of the needs of the marketplace and how Product N can fulfill those needs.

RELATED TASKS	Assigned To:	Defin-ed	Assign-ed	Due Date	Complet-ed
Conduct primary research (e.g. focus groups, surveys, etc.)					X
Purchase outside market research					X
Assemble market information for ease of use					
Comments: As indicated, the first two tasks have been completed, but the assemblage of the information for ease of use is only partially done and even this much needs to be redone and updated.					

The conclusion of the audit was that the client was in a low degree of readiness to launch *Product N*. There were just too many things that had not been addressed, had been addressed only partially or had to be addressed all over again. Up to the point of the engagement, only one of the readiness requirements had been completely met.

Another finding was that the resources assigned to the launch were inadequate for meeting the goals by the desired launch date. The comprehensiveness of the audit helped reveal just where the short falls were and gave justification for the allocation of additional resources.

Made in the USA
Monee, IL
20 June 2021

71796424R00090